PRAISE FOR *THE TRANSFORMATIVE POWER OF COLLABORATIVE INQUIRY*

"There is a new #1 in Visible Learning—teachers' collective efficacy. Thi. ~. gets to the heart of working together to build the confidence that teachers and school leaders can change the learning lives of all learners, that they then do change their learning lives, and that they collaborate in this endeavor. Donohoo and Velasco ensure we focus on the right problems to collaborate about, that the process can be scaled, and that thinking is provoked to maximize impact. A most worthwhile book that shows the why, the how, and the impact of collaborative inquiry."

—John Hattie, Professor of Education and
Director of the Melbourne Education Research Institute
University of Melbourne
Melbourne, Australia

"The concept of collaborative inquiry is increasingly bandied about these days with little precision. In one fell swoop Donohoo and Velasco change all that with this succinct, hard-hitting, complete, powerful, and above all accessible book on collaborative inquiry. It's all here: research, practice, theory, examples, and crystal-clear charts and guides to comprehension and deep action. We learn what high-quality professional learning is, and what it is not (13 comparisons); the six lynchpins of collaborative inquiry; and the distinction between professional development and professional learning. Each chapter starts with a 'cardwork map' that contains the four key ideas in each chapter. The Transformative Power of Collaborative Inquiry *is as it promises: you can transform learning in your school and district by examining and employing the ideas in this book!"*

—Michael Fullan, Professor Emeritus
OISE/University of Toronto
Toronto, Ontario

"The power of collaboration is evident throughout this book as Donohoo and Velasco guide readers through an inquiry process that can strengthen every professional learning community. They provide the 'how' to the oft-asked question about teacher collaboration and shine light on the path that will get us all there. Their goal is clear—learning—and they hold teachers in the highest esteem as they help us all improve our interactions with our peers to benefit students."

—Douglas Fisher, Professor
San Diego State University
San Diego, CA

"Perhaps the greatest lesson we can learn from The Transformative Power of Collaborative Inquiry *is that growth and development involve being open to challenges on the way to learning, leading, and authentic collaboration. This book is a must-read and a wonderful guide!"*

—Ann Lieberman, Senior Scholar
Stanford University
Palo Alto, CA

"By focusing on the importance of teachers as drivers for school improvement, Donohoo and Velasco highlight an important element that is often overlooked in this crucial learning process. Realizing that school improvement is not an event, they help us engage in the collaborative inquiry process in

a way that changes culture in schools, leading to improved outcomes for students. Teachers in classrooms, principals in schools, and leaders in central offices all play significant roles in creating the conditions for learning and improvement that are outlined in this very timely work."

—John Malloy, Director of Education
Toronto District School Board
Toronto, Ontario

"The Transformative Power of Collaborative Inquiry is a quest for educators to learn collaboratively in order to improve student achievement while improving individual and shared educational practices. It blends what collaborative inquiry is with researchers' work that supports the importance of inquiry as a productive mindset with practical tools, processes, and structures. Donohoo and Velasco build a case that collaborative inquiry can serve as a productive school improvement structure."

—Larry Thomas, Executive Director
Oakland Schools Michigan
Oakland County, MI

"Donohoo and Velasco's book provides an engaging, informed, and practical call to action for placing educators as the leaders of their own, their peers', and their students' learning through The Transformative Power of Collaborative Inquiry. Vitally, they go beyond merely calling for action to providing examples from schools and educators, from their own professional experiences, and from latest research evidence. There are many authors who advocate for collaborative inquiry; where Donohoo and Velasco stand out is in providing a timely must-read book with useful resources. These resources support facilitators in developing conditions and practices for quality collaborative inquiry, benefitting both educators and students."

—Carol Campbell, Associate Professor
Ontario Institute for Studies in Education, University of Toronto
Toronto, Ontario

"Robust and ongoing collaborative inquiry at every level—among teachers but also among school and system leaders—has been shown to improve schools and school systems. Yet such collaborative inquiry remains relatively uncommon. This book enables collaborative inquiry 'at scale' by combining an informed and nuanced grasp of relevant research with astute and practical guidance derived from the authors' own extensive experience."

—Judith Warren Little, Professor
University of California, Berkley
Berkley, CA

"The Transformative Power of Collaborative Inquiry is a fantastic resource for anyone interested in realizing the enormous potential of collaborative inquiry to substantially deepen the learning of students, adults, and educational systems. With a rich collection of guidelines, tools, and examples, Jenni Donohoo and Moses Velasco bring clarity and precision to the what, the how, and the why of effective collaborative inquiry. A valuable and timely book for change agents in schools and districts."

—Santiago Rincon-Gallardo, Banting Postdoctoral Fellow
Ontario Institute for Studies in Education
Toronto, Ontario

The Transformative Power of Collaborative Inquiry

The Transformative Power of Collaborative Inquiry

Realizing Change in Schools and Classrooms

Jenni Donohoo

Moses Velasco

A Joint Publication

FOR INFORMATION:

Corwin
A SAGE Company
2455 Teller Road
Thousand Oaks, California 91320
(800) 233-9936
www.corwin.com

SAGE Publications Ltd.
1 Oliver's Yard
55 City Road
London EC1Y 1SP
United Kingdom

SAGE Publications India Pvt. Ltd.
B 1/I 1 Mohan Cooperative Industrial Area
Mathura Road, New Delhi 110 044
India

SAGE Publications Asia-Pacific Pte. Ltd.
3 Church Street
#10-04 Samsung Hub
Singapore 049483

Program Director: Dan Alpert
Senior Associate Editor: Kimberly Greenberg
Editorial Assistant: Katie Crilley
Production Editor: Amy Schroller
Copy Editor: Karin Rathert
Typesetter: C&M Digitals (P) Ltd.
Proofreader: Laura Webb
Indexer: Karen Wiley
Cover Designer: Karine Hovsepian
Marketing Manager: Charline Maher

Library of Congress Cataloging-in-Publication Data

Names: Donohoo, Jenni, author. | Velasco, Moses, author.

Title: The transformative power of collaborative inquiry : realizing change in schools and classrooms / Jenni Donohoo, Moses Velasco.

Description: Thousand Oaks, California : Corwin, a SAGE Company, 2016. | Includes bibliographical references and index.

Identifiers: LCCN 2016004910 | ISBN 9781483383897 (pbk. : alk. paper)

Subjects: LCSH: Professional learning communities—United States. | Teachers—Professional relationships—United States. | School improvement programs—United States. | Educational change—United States. | Educational leadership—United States.

Classification: LCC LB1731 .D589 2016 | DDC 370.71/1—dc23
LC record available at https://lccn.loc.gov/2016004910

This book is printed on acid-free paper.

SUSTAINABLE FORESTRY INITIATIVE
Certified Chain of Custody
Promoting Sustainable Forestry
www.sfiprogram.org
SFI-01268
SFI label applies to text stock

16 17 18 19 20 10 9 8 7 6 5 4 3 2

Contents

List of Figures, Tables, and Resources   x

Preface   xii

Acknowledgments   xv

About the Authors   xvi

PART I COLLABORATIVE INQUIRY: A TRANSFORMATIVE PROFESSIONAL LEARNING DESIGN

1. Teacher-Driven Improvement   2

    Addressing Adaptive Challenges   5

    A Collaborative Inquiry Framework   6

    What It Is and What It Is Not   9

    What Do the Experts Say About Professional Learning?   13

    Moving Collaborative Inquiry From Theory to Practice   15

2. Bringing Collaborative Inquiry to Scale   17

    Coburn's (2003) Redefinition of Scale   18

    Conditions Necessary to Bring Collaborative Inquiry to Scale   19

      Lynchpin #1—Voluntary Participation   20

      Lynchpin #2—Shared Leadership   20

      Lynchpin #3—Guided From Experience   22

      Lynchpin #4—Achieved Coherence   25

      Lynchpin #5—Learning Is Recognized and Disseminated   26

      Lynchpin #6—Skilled Facilitation   27

PART II STRENGTHENING THE POWER: REALIZING CHANGE IN SCHOOLS AND CLASSROOMS

3. Determining and Maintaining a Focus   32

    Establishing a Needs-Based Focus   33

      Affective Student-Learning Needs   35

      Cognitive Student-Learning Needs   39

Metacognitive Student-Learning Needs 40

Considerations Regarding Multidisciplinary Teams 42

Formulating an Inquiry Question 44

Developing a Robust Theory of Action 44

Observations About Current Theories of Action 46

Developing a Theory of Action That Will Travel Well 47

Revisiting and Revising Theories of Action 50

4. **Provoking Thinking to Assess Impact** 52

Building Appreciation for and Capacity to
Use a Variety of Assessment Data 53

Types of Data That Can Be Used for School Improvement 54

Factors That Influence Data Collection 57

Teacher Learning Through the Collaborative
Analysis of Student Work 59

Strategies for Examining Student Work 61

Determining Next Best Move 63

The Results Path 63

Reconciling Discrepancies: Theories of Action 65

Extending Thinking About Practice Through Reflection 67

Changing the Conversation 71

5. **Shaping the Development
of a Professional Learning Culture** 73

Shifting From Professional
Development to Professional Learning 74

Unpack the Differences: Professional
Development and Professional Learning 75

Make Explicit the Relationship Between Change and Learning 77

Long-Term Commitment 78

Building Quality Professional Relationships 80

Knight's Partnership Principles
Applied to Collaborative Inquiry 81

Principle #1—Equality 81

Principle #2—Choice 81

Principle #3—Voice 82

Principle #4—Reflection 82

Principle #5—Dialogue 82

Principle #6—Praxis 83

Principle #7—Reciprocity 83

The Role of Trust   83

Improving Collaboration   85

    Developing the Team   86

    Cocreating Norms for Interaction   89

    Navigating Conflict   91

Expanding the Reach of Learning   93

Strategies to Expand the Reach of Learning   93

    Establish Networks   93

    Create Online Spaces for Collaborations   94

    Host a Learning Fair   96

    Host a Facilitator Summit   97

    Encourage Publication and Opportunities for Presentations   97

Resources   **101**

References   **107**

Index   **113**

List of Figures, Tables, and Resources

Figures

Figure 1.1   Collaborative Inquiry as
              Transformative Professional Learning   2

Figure 1.2   A Collaborative Inquiry Framework   7

Figure 2.1   Wider and Deeper Adoption of Collaborative Inquiry 17

Figure 3.1   Determining and Maintaining a Focus   32

Figure 3.2   Black Box/Glass Box   48

Figure 4.1   Provoking Thinking to Assess Impact   52

Figure 4.2   Results Path   64

Figure 4.3   Resource B—Reflecting on Practice   68

Figure 4.4   Resource C—Reflecting on Theories of Action   69

Figure 4.5   Resource D—Identifying the Gap:
              Practice and Values   70

Figure 5.1   Shaping the Development of
              a Professional Learning Culture   73

Tables

Table 1.1   Technical Fixes and Adaptive Challenges   5

Table 1.2   Collaborative Inquiry: What It Is and What It Is Not 11

Table 5.1   Differences Between Professional
             Development and Professional Learning   76

Table 5.2   The Relationship Between Change and Learning   78

Table 5.3   Facilitator Knowledge and
             Skills for Team Development   86

Table 5.4   Individual Stances Determining Team Investment 88

Table 5.5   Dynamic Tensions: A Framework
             for the Cocreation of Norms   90

Resources

Resource A   Questions to Strengthen Evidence Collection   101

Resource B   Reflecting on Practice   103

Resource C   Reflecting on Theories of Action   104

Resource D   Identifying the Gap: Practice and
              Values Assessment *for* Learning   105

Preface

Collaborative inquiry is a powerful design for professional learning that supports the notion of teacher leadership as it recognizes the role of teachers in ongoing school improvement. It provides a systematic approach for educators to identify professional dilemmas and determine resolutions through shared inquiry, problem-solving, and reflection. As educators uncover and negotiate differences and similarities in beliefs about what constitutes deep learning and effective practice, they learn new ways of working together and develop collective efficacy. Rather than being merely consumers of research and the professional knowledge that accompanies it, educators who engage in collaborative inquiry become producers and disseminators of knowledge.

By utilizing collaborative inquiry as an approach to professional learning, educators develop the adaptive capacity to address and overcome difficult challenges they face everyday. The ability to address student-learning needs no longer depends on individuals but on the collective wisdom brought by a team of educators with diverse experiences and expertise. Challenges are addressed through a coordinated and collective effort, which helps to ensure greater success for *all* students. Inquiry becomes a broader strategy to transform the culture of a school and school district.

There are ongoing challenges however, in moving collaborative inquiry from theory to practice. This book provides insights for educators who are interested in supporting and/or facilitating an inquiry approach to system learning by exploring the benefits and hurdles and implications for administrators, teachers, and students. It identifies and addresses the conditions needed to bring about a wider and deeper adoption of collaborative inquiry and contains observations to help prevent collaborative inquiry from being adopted superficially. In addressing how to bring collaborative inquiry to scale, lessons learned from the field are included so that school leaders can learn from each other's experiences.

This book does not provide step-by-step instructions for engaging in an inquiry cycle. Rather, it moves beyond a focus on how to *do* inquiry. In examining the conditions necessary to support collaborative inquiry, insights for strengthening the work are provided. In this book, readers will find

- A rationale and framework for engaging in inquiry
- A description of the conditions that are vital to ensuring collaborative inquiry reaches scale
- A needs-based focus defined
- Ways to strengthen theories of action
- Ideas to provoke thinking to assess impact
- Ways to strategically build a professional learning culture

Theories of action are used to explain specific changes intended to improve professional practice. They serve to help understand behavior, expose thinking and reasons behind actions, and are essential in clarifying strategies for change. We have borrowed Bushe's (2010) "Cardwork Strategy" in order to gain clarity about our theories of action and to make them more explicit to the reader. A cardwork is a way of capturing a theory of action and contains a title, a subtitle, and three or four phrases connected by a spinning propeller (Bushe, 2010, p. 166). While the title describes what the theory is about, the subtitle articulates the outcomes of successful actions, and the phrases indicate a complete theory of how to reach that outcome. The purpose of the spinning propeller is to show that the critical aspects are not necessarily accomplished in a step-by-step sequence but rather they "spin" to demonstrate a more fluid approach.

Readers will find the following cardwork maps that describe our theories of action at the start of each chapter:

- Collaborative Inquiry as Transformative Professional Learning: Realizing Change in Schools and Classrooms
- Wider and Deeper Adoption of Collaborative Inquiry: Bringing Collaborative Inquiry to Scale
- Determining and Maintaining a Focus: Teams Invest in What Matters the Most
- Provoking Thinking to Assess Impact: Educators Have a Clear Understanding of How their Actions Impact Student Outcomes
- Shaping the Development of a Professional Learning Culture: Inquiry and Collaboration Are Habits of Mind

Our purpose in writing this book was to refine the knowledge base of collaborative inquiry. Our hope is that educators take the stance of professional inquirers, embody the qualities of lifelong learners, and foster professional learning cultures where engagement in deep and impactful problem-solving is a habit of mind. Educators will find this book helpful as they navigate the hurdles that surface as they come together to learn in new and different ways. Our intention is to help leaders "stay the course," so that collaborative inquiry can live up to what it promises—transformations in learning, leading, and teaching.

Acknowledgments

We would like to thank all of the educators we have worked with as they engaged in collaborative inquiry over the last few years. Thank you for inviting us to be part of the process and allowing us to study and learn alongside you. The rich conversations we have had with teachers, department heads, and administrators enabled us to think deeply about the structures and processes needed to support professional learning. This book was largely driven by the questions that individuals and teams posed as they embraced the design of collaborative inquiry and worked through the process in order to better support students' learning needs.

We have benefited greatly from collaborating with educators including our colleagues on the Toronto District School Board, professors from the Ontario Institute for Studies in Education (OISE), the Curriculum and Assessment Policy Branch at the Ministry of Education in Ontario, and Corwin Authors and Consultants. We would especially like to thank our colleagues and friends from Learning Forward. Even though we only see each other once or twice a year, our professional and personal lives are enriched as a result.

We would like thank Dan Alpert, our editor, who has been incredibly supportive, along with many amazing people in the Corwin family, including Mike Soules, Lisa Shaw, and Kristin Anderson.

We would also like to acknowledge Becky Allen, Julie Balen, Marty Chaffee, Patricia Chinn, Simon Feasey, Gillian Hall, Sandy Homb, Jim Lalik, Dean Maltby, and Patrick Miller for being willing to share their experiences related to supporting and scaling collaborative inquiry.

Finally, Jenni would like to thank her husband, Jim for his unwavering support and confidence.

Moses would like to thank Andrea Payne for being an incredible sounding board and a fantastic partner in advancing teacher leadership.

About the Authors

 **Jenni Donohoo** is a research and program evaluation consultant working on secondment as a provincial literacy lead in the Curriculum and Assessment Policy Branch in the Ontario Ministry of Education. Jenni has a doctorate in education and her areas of expertise include adolescent literacy, metacognition, feedback and assessment, and supporting professional learning communities. She teaches an additional qualification course online through the University of Windsor and is the past president of Learning Forward Ontario. Jenni is also a best-selling author and consultant for Corwin. She lives with her husband and their two golden retrievers in a 175-year-old home in historic Amherstburg, Ontario. Jenni and Jim spend most of their spare time arguing about how to renovate their heritage home.

 **Moses Velasco** is a professional learning leader with Toronto District School Board. He has held several teacher leadership positions at both the school level and central departments. He is currently completing a masters of education degree with the Ontario Institute for Studies in Education (OISE) at the University of Toronto. In addition to his professional and academic work, he sits on the board of directors for the Learning Forward Ontario affiliate. Moses is passionate about the critical role teachers play in improving education by expanding their understanding and exercise of leadership and influence. He also loves karaoke.

Part I

Collaborative Inquiry

A Transformative
Professional Learning Design

1 Teacher-Driven Improvement

"Changing teaching means changing the understanding that underlies the teaching" (Katz & Dack, 2013, p. 5).

Figure 1.1 Collaborative Inquiry as Transformative Professional Learning

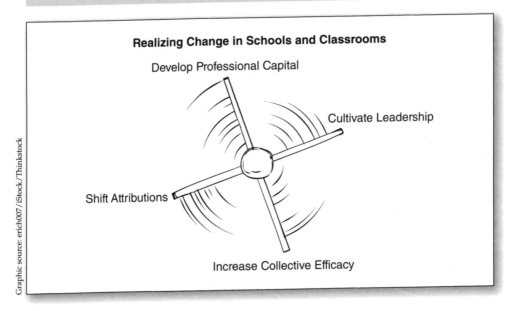

Realizing Change in Schools and Classrooms

Develop Professional Capital

Cultivate Leadership

Shift Attributions

Increase Collective Efficacy

Graphic source: erich007/iStock/Thinkstock

Collaborative inquiry holds the potential to transform learning, leading, and teaching. This is confirmed in research and our work with teams, schools, and districts. Powerful professional learning designs are grounded in educator's practice, inquiry oriented, and collaborative and reflective in nature. Collaborative inquiry provides a structure for educators to lead and learn together productively. It is an instrumental approach to developing teacher leadership and professional capital, increasing efficacy, and shifting attributions regarding causes for students' success or failure. In moving the "learning of teaching closer to practice" (Gallimore, Ermeling, Saunders, & Goldenberg, 2009, p. 538), conversations change from what has been *taught* to what has been *learned*.

We have witnessed a growing and deep appreciation for the transformative changes that collaborative inquiry can deliver. Many teachers have reported that engaging in collaborative inquiry has not only impacted their teaching practices but also how they understand and value ongoing, relevant, and collaborative professional learning. School administrators echo these sentiments when they share how teachers engaged in collaborative inquiry speak with excitement about their learning in a way that is infectious and felt throughout the school. All agree that when teachers are learning, students' learning experiences are enhanced.

The transformative potential of collaborative inquiry is also reflected in the relationship between collaboration, inquiry, and efficacy. Efficacy matters. Eells (2011) examined the relationship between collective teacher efficacy and student achievement. Results from this meta-analysis demonstrated that when educators believe that together they can make a difference, the impact on student gains can almost quadruple. Hattie (2009) synthesized over 800 meta-analyses that examined various factors impacting student achievement. Hattie continues to update this synthesis and recently ranked collective teacher efficacy as the number *one* factor influencing student achievement (personal communication, November 19, 2015). Studies show that teacher's self-efficacy and collective efficacy increase when teachers collaborate (Beauchamp, Klassen, Parsons, Durksen, & Taylor, 2014; Horton & Martin, 2013; Johnson, 2012; Little, 1990; Moolenaar, Sleegers, & Daly, 2012). Studies also show that when collaborative teams engage in inquiry self-efficacy increases (Bruce & Flynn, 2013; Cooper-Twamley, 2009; Galligan, 2011; Henson, 2001). In addition,

> "A major consequence of collaborative inquiry is collective efficacy—a sense that teachers can overcome learning challenges when they rely on one another's expertise" (Colton, Langer, & Goff, 2016, p. 21).

> Teacher self-efficacy is a teacher's belief that he or she has the ability to influence student learning (Bandura, 1997).

> In schools, collective efficacy refers to educators' beliefs that together they can organize and execute the "action required to have a positive effect on students" (Goddard, Hoy, & Woolfolk Hoy, 2003, p. 4).

Voelkel Jr. (2011) demonstrated a positive relationship between collective effi-cacy and professional learning communities characterized by collaboration and inquiry.

Gallimore et al. (2009) provided evidence that the inquiry process also helps to bring about changes in attributions. This research demonstrated a shift in attributions of improved student performance to teaching rather than external causes. Instead of attributing student success and/or failure to factors outside of their control, teachers came to better understand their ability to impact student outcomes. The authors noted that teachers shifted from assumptions that included "I planned and taught the lesson, but they didn't get it" to "you haven't taught it until they've learned" as a result of engaging in a collaborative inquiry process.

While the transformation of learning, leading, and teaching rests with *all* educators, the role and position of teachers in school improvement can-not be overlooked or understated. Hargreaves and Fullan (2012) made this sobering observation:

> When the classroom door is closed, the teacher will always remain in charge. Where students are concerned, the teacher will always be more powerful than the principal, the president, or the prime minister. Successful and sustainable improvement can therefore never be done *to or even for* teachers. It can only ever be achieved *by and with* them. (p. 45)

Collaborative inquiry is a process that recognizes and values teach-ers as drivers for school improvement, as opposed to be being the targets of improvement. It provides a systematic approach for teachers to explore issues and determine resolutions through shared inquiry, reflection, and dialogue. Rather than being merely consumers of research and the professional knowledge that accompanies it, teachers engaged in collaborative inquiry become producers and disseminators of knowledge.

Through the collaborative inquiry process, teachers develop profes-sional capital as described by Hargreaves and Fullan (2012). In recasting the teacher's role in improvement efforts, the authors advocate for the development of professional capital that includes human capital (the tal-ent of individuals), social capital (the collaborative power of the group), and decisional capital (the wisdom and expertise to make sound judg-ments about learners that are cultivated over many years) (p. 5). Professional capital is not something that is bestowed upon educators but rather unleashed within and through them when they engage in a cycle of inquiry. The understanding and definition of teacher leadership expands, and teachers become leaders of their learning.

ADDRESSING ADAPTIVE CHALLENGES

Collaborative inquiry marries professional learning and leadership to simultaneously surface and transform the way student learning is understood and planned for. Since these transformations are manifested in teaching behaviors and beliefs, the challenges accompanying the changes can be described as adaptive in nature. Adaptive challenges are difficult to resolve, as solutions require new learning and upset past ways of doing things. Heifetz, Grashow, and Linsky (2009) pointed out that there is no clear path to solving an adaptive challenge. Solutions are iterative and appear more elusive as they challenge the status quo and existing cultures that may foster resistance. Collaborative inquiry can be understood as a promising way to address adaptive challenges in education. It is powerful because it transforms the learning of teachers by letting them lead their professional learning in ways that address the adaptive challenges of the classroom.

> Technical problems are typically easy to identify and require quick solutions. They are usually solved by an authority or expert, and people are generally receptive, as the solution only requires changes in one or two areas. When technical problems are solved, compliance tends to be the outcome. The intended outcome of collaborative inquiry, however, is not compliance but rather teacher commitment to being innovative in the improvement of their practices. Approaches in addressing adaptive challenges are needed to reach this very different outcome.

The single biggest failure of leadership is applying a technical fix to an adaptive challenge (Heifetz & Laurie, 1997).

Table 1.1 Technical Fixes and Adaptive Challenges

Technical Fixes	Adaptive Challenges
Administering a practice test to prepare students for annual standardized literacy tests	Helping content-area teachers integrate literacy instruction into their everyday practice
Increasing the penalty for late or missing work	Raising awareness of ineffective grading practice
Sending students for resource support	Differentiating instruction to meet students' readiness levels
Substituting technology for tasks that could be done with or without it	Integrating technology in support of student-centered, problem-based learning

A COLLABORATIVE INQUIRY FRAMEWORK

There are numerous collaborative inquiry frameworks, and the one proposed in this book does not differ significantly from others. In fact, it is a slight modification to Timperley, Wilson, Barrar, and Fung's (2007) teacher inquiry cycle. Ideas that draw upon Timperley, Kaser, and Halbert's (2014) revised spiral of inquiry are also reflected in this book. In addition, as we continue to learn and refine *our practice* as we support collaborative inquiry in school districts, the ideas suggested in one of the author's earlier works entitled *Collaborative Inquiry for Educators: A Facilitator's Guide to School Improvement* are expanded upon.

The collaborative inquiry cycle is situated within the work of a professional learning community. The process begins with teams identifying a needs-based focus. Once a *learning* need is identified, the team develops an inquiry question that they are genuinely curious about. Teams begin to map out a theory of action in order to identify assumptions and strengthen and share their theorizing. During this process, the team identifies educators' learning needs. A driving question the team asks is, "What classroom and/or leadership practices (that are different from what we are currently doing) could we learn more about to address the gaps in student learning that we have identified?" Once participants identify and articulate their own learning needs, they engage in professional learning in order to deepen professional knowledge and refine skills.

Figure 1.2 illustrates different ways in which educators might engage in learning throughout the cycle. While not every avenue that leads to new understandings is depicted in the illustration, the point is that participants are provided the autonomy to pursue a model of learning that best fits the needs they have identified. If a participant needs to understand how to support inquiry-based learning in their classroom, peer observation might be an appropriate starting point. If a participant needs to understand how to utilize instructional time in order to maximize consolidation of learning, he or she might engage in lesson study. If a team member determines he needs to improve questioning skills, he might invite a coach into his classroom. If participants need to better understand strategies for increasing metacognition, they might access research or reach out to an expert in the field. Alternatively, participants might seek opportunities for direct instruction, depending on the learning need identified. These methods of learning are not in competition with the inquiry but are in aid of finding a solution to the inquiry posed.

New practices are tested and, collectively, teams examine artifacts representative of students' learning. The team considers the impact of the changes on student outcomes before determining next steps. Notice the arrow circles back from "Determine next best move" to "Deepen

Figure 1.2 A Collaborative Inquiry Framework

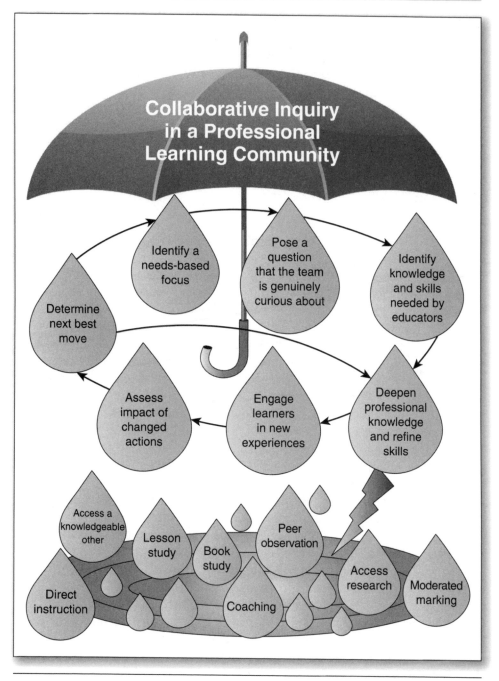

Adapted from *Teacher Professional Learning and Development Best Evidence Synthesis Iteration*, Timperley, Wilson, Barrar, and Fung (2007).

professional knowledge and refine skills." It is likely that teams will cycle back a number of times, as they test and learn more about new and different approaches. The number of iterations usually depends on the willingness and timeliness in which teams examine evidence. If teams adopt a *wait and see* outlook, then it is less likely inquiries will be sustained. In order to make responsive changes and adjust instruction accordingly, teams need to examine student evidence frequently. This is discussed at greater length in Chapter 4. The cycle moves to a new iteration when team members feel they are able to answer the question posed at the beginning of the cycle. The process of documenting the team's learning (including recommendations for others) encourages further reflection and helps to consolidate understanding. Recognition and celebration are integral to a team's engagement in subsequent cycles.

A Flexible and Applicable Approach to Learning

Hopkins Public Schools was seeking a process to better guide educators in seeking answers to student learning challenges. Despite teachers routinely using information from formative assessments to respond to student learning needs and implementing many interventions in classrooms, including school-wide programs, educators were frustrated with the minimal gains in assessment scores. Teachers recognized that students needed more than just content to be successful. Additionally, educators in nontraditional classrooms were looking for a process that would better fit the needs of their work.

In response, Becky Allen, staff development coordinator, and Sandy Homb, Q-Comp manager, offered collaborative inquiry as an option to the existing Professional Learning Community (PLC) process. Teacher leaders provided training and support as nearly 40 percent of PLCs opted to use collaborative inquiry the first year it was offered. Through a series of five face-to-face sessions, teams were guided in developing their inquiry question, theory of action, evidence collection plan, and the use of tools for examining evidence.

Based on this process, PLCs pursued a wide array of questions in an effort to determine how to increase engagement and build student skills, such as independence, literacy skills, technology integration, and problem-solving skills. This process was also a welcomed opportunity for staff working directly with adults and those working with students outside of a traditional classroom. A pretest/posttest model did not fit well with measuring the impact of their practices, and this process allowed for a variety of tools to answer questions about providing support to staff, families, or individual students.

Teachers who engaged in this process have found collaborative inquiry to be applicable and flexible for their needs. A critical part of the evidence collection process centered around gathering data pertaining to their own practice. This created a reflective environment and purposeful dialogue among colleagues. The inquiry process is personal; teams pursued questions that were significant and required them to measure the impact of their practices. Collaborative inquiry worked because teachers inquired into their own problems of practice and used a research process that was relevant and meaningful to their daily work.

WHAT IT IS AND WHAT IT IS NOT

Collaborative inquiry is first and foremost a design for high quality professional learning that recognizes and celebrates the critical role of educators in improving student outcomes. While stages of the process share similarities to research designs, the intent is not for collaborative inquiry teams to undertake rigorous experimental research. Hattie (cited in Stewart, 2015) cautioned that teachers should not be expected to conduct research in schools or classrooms, noting that teachers are busy enough and that research skills are acquired through specialized graduate courses. Hattie prefers teachers not be researchers, but they be evaluators. Hattie (2012) also noted that "we need to collaborate to build a team working together to solve the dilemmas in learning, to collectively share and critique the nature and quality of evidence that shows our impact on student learning" (p. 151). Hattie's latter statement is reflective of the activities of a collaborative inquiry team.

Rather than trying to randomly assign students to a control group and/or an experimental group while trying to control for variables and put interventions in place, collaborative inquiry teams engage in the following activities: identifying the knowledge and skills students need in order to succeed; investigating and selecting promising practices to address students' needs; learning more about these practices by testing them in their classrooms; and assessing the impact of their actions in order to determine next steps. The cycle is repeated as educators reflect on and adapt their instruction based on a collective and careful examination of evidence.

This approach to professional learning is notably different from traditional models that were often based on isolated topics, determined and prioritized by others, and thus lacking connections with real problems experienced by classroom educators. Collaborative inquiry is driven by a central question composed by team members and based on perplexing issues related to learning and teaching. Solutions are determined by team members and, while the process honors the professionalism of the participants, their decisions should be informed by evidence, research on promising practices, and/or knowledgeable others. Decisions are not based on hunches; there is too much at stake.

People learn new ways of working together as they provide support to one another during each stage of the process. They bring unique experiences and share their expertise for the benefit of the team as they co-construct understanding and create new knowledge. Together, they problem solve and develop solutions to address adaptive challenges in order to ensure that students' needs are met. Learning is solidified as team members identify, articulate, and reflect on the incongruence between espoused theories of action and theories-in-use. Teachers lead and learn *with* and *from* each other. Shared ownership for school improvement and a sense of collective efficacy often results.

> Espoused theories of action refer to the values and beliefs that people believe guide their behavior. Theories-in-use are the values and beliefs that are actually reflected in people's behaviors. Argyris and Schön (1978) noted that few people are aware of their theories-in-use or that theories-in-use are not always the same as the theories they espouse.

Collaborative inquiry is a powerful strategy for building teachers' capacity to lead, because it provides a structure for teachers to become authentic leaders and decision makers. Leadership opportunities extend beyond merely serving on a committee or acting as a department or grade level chair. Through their collaborative work and *learning by doing*, teachers have the potential to become more meaningfully involved in school improvement and catalysts for change.

Katz, Earl, and Ben Jaafar (2009) noted that "for inquiry to be truly effective, it needs to become a way of doing business, a way of thinking, a *habit of mind*, rather than a discrete event" (p. 43). Dweck's (2006) work helped to uncover the power of people's *habits of mind* and how they impact our actions—even if we are unaware of them. The beliefs we hold are very powerful and our actions are guided by these beliefs. Hattie (2012) presented a set of mindframes that "underpin our every action and decision in a school" (p. 159). Mindframes relate to how we think, and the specific mindframes that teachers have about their role is critical. Hattie (2012) suggested that "the most powerful way of thinking about a teacher's role is for teachers to see themselves as evaluators of their effects on students" (p. 14). During a collaborative inquiry cycle, team members examine the link between the actions of educators and student results. Teams gather evidence that helps to inform, modify, or maintain evaluation beliefs about their effects.

> "The ultimate goal of engaging in the process is to create an inquiry stance toward teaching. This stance becomes a professional positioning, where questioning one's own practice becomes part of an educator's work and eventually part of the district culture" (Fichtman Dana, Thomas, & Boynton, 2011, p. 11).

Engaging in collaborative inquiry is often described by participants as both risky and rewarding. It is risky because educators are hesitant to admit they do not have all the answers. Katz et al. (2009) call this psychological condition the "imposter syndrome" (p. 91). They refer to it as "an inner voice" that whispers "I have no idea how it is that I came to be doing what I'm doing but hopefully nobody will find me out!" (p. 91). Opening up our practices to scrutiny is very risky for some, but it is also very rewarding. Csikszentmihalyi (1990) noted that "periods of struggling to overcome challenges are what people find to be the most enjoyable times of their lives" (p. 6). It is rewarding, because once new insight is gained, participants realize the effort was worthwhile. Educators are empowered as they work together to solve the challenges they face in their day-to-day practice. They recognize the power of the team and increased efficacy results.

Finally, the process is often referred to as "muddy," as participants experience a certain amount of ambiguity. Educators are not used to being provided the freedom to direct their own professional learning, and they are often unclear as to where their inquiries will lead them. As noted earlier, there is no clear path when solving an adaptive challenge. People will experience disequilibrium, but as Katz and Dack (2013) noted, "the experience of cognitive discomfort is not an unfortunate consequence of new learning; it is an essential prerequisite of new learning" (p. 20). As teams work their way through the adaptive challenge, the path becomes less ambiguous.

> Disequilibrium is potentially generated when a leader raises issues or asks questions that disturb people—forcing them to come to terms with points of view or problems that they would rather not consider (Heifetz et al., 2009).

Table 1.2   Collaborative Inquiry: What It Is and What It Is Not

What It Is	What It Is Not
A high quality professional learning design	Experimental research design
A cyclical and iterative process for improving student learning and teaching practices	Linear or lock step, a checklist of actions
Based on issues related to the learning needs of the students of the participating educators	Based on topics that determined/prioritized by someone other than the classroom educator

(Continued)

Table 1.2 (Continued)

What It Is	What It Is Not
Driven by a central question—in which the answer is unknown to participants	Based on a topic mandated by administrators or central office staff
Adaptive in nature as new knowledge is generated amongst team members	The transmission of knowledge from central office personnel or outside experts
Steered in a direction determined by participants	Directed by outside experts
Facilitated from within—by members of the team	Facilitated by outside experts
Decisions informed by evidence, research on promising practices, and/or the advice of experts	"Cherry picking" teaching approaches
The deep implementation of new and different approaches to classroom instruction	More of the same while expecting different results
Gathering a variety of evidence—collectively examined at multiple points (not excluding pretest and posttest data)	Pretest, posttest data—examined at the beginning and end of the semester or at the beginning and end of the school year
A mindset, a way of thinking, a belief that what we do matters and that we need to evaluate the effects of our actions on student learning and achievement	A mindset, a way of thinking, a belief that no matter what we do, we cannot reach all students, having no appreciation for self-assessment
Risky, rewarding, empowering	Risk-free nor unhelpful
Sometimes a "muddy" process	A clearly laid out path

Developing New Understandings and Overcoming Challenges

Julie Balen, teacher at Wikwemikong High School in Ontario, is working to help students overcome many challenges. Julie and her colleagues in the English department utilize collaborative inquiry as an approach to professional learning, so that they can identify what it is they need to know and be able to do in order to better serve their students. Julie noted that the collaborative inquiry process has helped her come to a new understanding about self-directed learning. It has given her the freedom to innovate and take risks without negative consequences and has taught her that the learning from one collaborative inquiry prepares the ground for the new learning that will emerge in the next one. It is this recursiveness, both within a collaborative inquiry and between collaborative inquiries, that is so powerful. In addition, it has made visible student-learning needs that were either not recognized in the past or were taken for granted.

WHAT DO THE EXPERTS SAY ABOUT PROFESSIONAL LEARNING?

When reviewing numerous books, articles, and reports written over the past few of decades by leading education experts, about systemic change and the transformative potential of professional development, three themes permeate: teacher leadership, collaboration, and inquiry.

Little (1982) concluded that staff development appeared to have greatest influence where there was a "prevailing norm of analysis, evaluation, and experimentation" (p. 339). Based on research surrounding workplace conditions of school success, Little (1982) suggested that the focus on professional improvement be at an organizational level rather than "an individual enterprise," (p. 338) noting that continuous improvement was a shared undertaking in schools that were the most adaptable and successful amongst those studied. Little (1990) also pointed out that collaboration was a powerful way to change teaching practice when it involved joint work, including critical inquiry, sustained scrutiny of practice, analysis, and debate in search of improvement.

Darling-Hammond (1998) pointed out that an optimum setting for teacher learning would provide opportunities for inquiry; where teachers try, test, talk about, and evaluate the results of learning and teaching. Darling-Hammond (1998) concluded that professional development strategies that succeeded in improving teaching were "grounded in participants' questions, inquiry, and experimentation" (p. 11) and "collaborative, involving a sharing of knowledge amongst educators" (p. 11). Also in the 1990's, Ball and Cohen (1999) made a case for collaborative inquiry as they proposed new ways to "understand and use practice as a site for professional learning, as well as ways to cultivate the sorts of inquiry into practice from which many teachers could learn" (p. 6). The authors suggested that if teaching and learning how to teach became the object of continuing and thoughtful inquiry, then "much of teachers' everyday work could become a source for constructive professional development"

(p. 6). Like the model suggested in this book, Ball and Cohen (1999) were not arguing that teachers should become researchers. Rather, they argued that "a stance of inquiry should be central to the role of teacher" (p. 11). The authors also noted that professional learning should be a collective endeavour, recognizing that creating and sustaining an inquiry-oriented stance is a "social enterprise" (p. 17).

In 2004, Lieberman and Miller promoted the role of teacher leadership in reshaping school culture and outlined a set of perspectives and practices that had the potential to transform teaching and schools. The transformative shifts included moving from "individualism to professional community" (p. 11) and from "technical and managed work to inquiry and leadership" (p. 11). Lieberman and Miller (2004) advocated for opportunities for teachers to "learn in practice" (p. 21) and "create knowledge rather than merely apply it" (p. 14). Reeves (2008) made similar arguments for reframing teacher leadership and offered a framework in which teachers "ask important questions, conduct investigations, discern inferences, and share their wisdom with colleagues" (p. 9). In 2010, Reeves studied school improvement plans and found nine characteristics that had measurable and significant effects on gains in student achievement. The inquiry process, where causal relationships between teaching and leadership practices and student results were identified as part of the school improvement plan, was one of the nine characteristics in successful schools.

Hargreaves and Fullan (2012) and Hattie (2012) also promoted inquiry as a valuable model for teacher learning. Hargreaves and Fullan (2012) suggested that "constant inquiry and continuous individual and collective development are essential to success" (p. 22) and noted that "teams, and communities are far more powerful than individuals when it comes to developing human capital" (p. 3). In addition, Hattie (2012) noted that a community of teachers who "work together to ask the questions, evaluate their impact, and decide on optimal next steps" (p. vii) is what is needed in order to advance education.

The Best Evidence Synthesis Iteration: Teacher Professional Learning and Development (Timperley et al., 2007) called for an "ongoing commitment to collaborative inquiry into the links between learning and teaching" (p. xxi). Building on this report, Timperley et al. (2014) proposed that "through a disciplined approach to collaborative inquiry, resulting in new learning and new action, that educators, learners, their families and involved community members will gain the confidence, the insights, and the mindsets required to design new and powerful learning systems" (p. 4). Katz et al. (2009) also specifically named collaborative inquiry as a way to "challenge the status quo" and an enabler of the "kind of professional learning that contributes to changed practice" (p. 46). Katz and

Dack (2013) suggested that *"collaborative inquiry* that challenges thinking and practice is the *how* of professional learning. It's the methodology for moving a learning focus forward" (p. 39).

There is a wealth of documentation, written over the past few decades, demonstrating that the most respected thought-leaders in education believe in the power of collaborative inquiry. There is also documented evidence to show its impact on transforming learning, leading, and teaching. Our concern is that collaborative inquiry will be abandoned, like many other impactful reform approaches that were poorly understood and inadequately supported. This book shares lessons learned from the field so that school leaders can learn from other's experiences. Too often change initiatives are abandoned during the early implementation phase. This book will help leaders stay the course, so collaborative inquiry can live up to what it promises—transformations in learning, leading, and teaching.

MOVING COLLABORATIVE INQUIRY FROM THEORY TO PRACTICE

Collaborative inquiry remains largely theoretical in many districts; a promise to transform leadership structures and the learning of educators and students. The ongoing challenge, however, has been bringing collaborative inquiry out of the realm of theory into the professional learning practices of educators. While collaborative inquiry has the potential to transform school improvement, simply putting structures in place for teams to come together and inquire about their practice is not enough to realize the transformation. Giving teachers time and resources to collaborate does not mean that they have the knowledge and desire to meaningfully do so. Yet, if this assumption is naively made, collaborative inquiry, as a result, will not be consistently adopted with fidelity.

If *adopted* as envisioned in this book, by engaging in the process, the quality of leadership will be cultivated in each and every individual. The term *adopted* was purposefully selected in favor of the overused and under established term *implemented*. The implementation of initiatives has been proven to be problematic in education. In addition, the term *implementation* implies the "deployment of a plan," and that plan usually belongs to someone else. The term *adopted* implies that something has been "embraced, taken on, or that an attitude or position has been assumed," and that is our hope for educators in regard to collaboratively inquiring into their practice. Every educator deserves access to high quality professional learning. Collaborative inquiry is a high quality design that is based on the premise that teachers are essential leaders in school improvement efforts. We hope that participants experience the richness in learning and leading that is afforded by the process.

In addressing this adaptive challenge, successful adoption must be measured in terms of whether teachers comfortably contest the status quo of their teaching practices, in addition to the assumptions and beliefs that frame and perpetuate those practices. This book was written for district and school leaders (administrators and teachers), as they support teams engaged in the adopting, refining, and sustaining collaborative inquiry. It is about moving beyond a focus of how to *do* inquiry. The purpose of this book is twofold:

1. To strengthen understanding of the conditions and qualities within the collaborative inquiry cycle that support ongoing educator learning and development.

2. To provide insight into the key considerations for a systemic approach that results in a full and vigorous adoption of collaborative inquiry.

The following themes will be explored in this book underscoring its twofold purpose:

- Bringing collaborative inquiry to scale
- Establishing and maintaining a needs-based focus
- Provoking thinking to assess impact
- Shaping the development of a professional learning culture

Ultimately, we envision collaborative inquiry as an alternative to short-term, top-down, formulaic approaches to professional learning that do not hold enough rigor to realize self-sustaining cycles of improvement in schools. In order for education to remain relevant and responsive to the current and future learning needs of students, teachers and other educational leaders must have mechanisms and processes in place to collaboratively identify how schools should improve and how to meaningfully refine and sustain those changes. Collaborative inquiry holds the potential to do that by calling each individual in education to raise within themselves a truer sense of leader and learner.

. . . .

Ultimately, we envision collaborative inquiry as an alternative to short-term, top-down, formulaic approaches to professional learning that do not hold enough rigor to realize self-sustaining cycles of improvement in schools.

. . . .

2 Bringing Collaborative Inquiry to Scale

"There is no way that a system will make an overall difference to student achievement by working one teacher at a time. Instead, the onus needs to be on everyone working collectively to improve student achievement" (Hattie, 2015, p. 5).

Figure 2.1 Wider and Deeper Adoption of Collaborative Inquiry

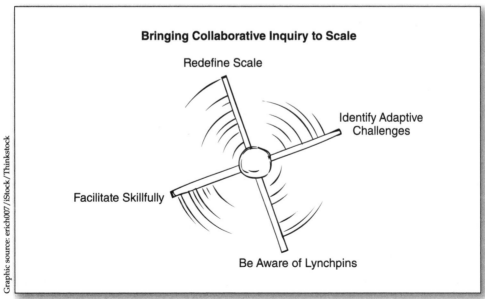

Bringing Collaborative Inquiry to Scale

Redefine Scale

Identify Adaptive Challenges

Facilitate Skillfully

Be Aware of Lynchpins

Graphic source: erich007 /iStock/Thinkstock

L eading educational researchers promote professional learning that is collaborative, encourages educators to inquire into problems of practice, apply new approaches and reflect on the results, and build collective knowledge. Collaborative inquiry as a scalable reform holds the potential to transform education systems. Adaptive challenges are identified and addressed when educators engage in collaborative inquiry, as the process necessitates the reconstruction of beliefs about the nature of learning, leading, and teaching. In addition to reframing teacher leadership, collaborative inquiry builds efficacy. When educators collaborate and develop solutions to address their problems of practice, efficacy increases. Research indicates that collective teacher efficacy is the number *one* factor that impacts student achievement (Hattie, personal communication, November 19, 2015).

Ensuring collaborative inquiry lives up to its potential will require a concerted effort, as collaborative inquiry teams can either "work together to either reinvent and improve teaching practice or simply reinforce the status quo" (Stanley, 2011, p. 73). Emihovich and Battaglia (2000) noted that the creativity and knowledge to begin this work is not lacking and that much of the work has already been initiated. What they suggest is lacking, however, is "the energy, discipline, and patience to study what is involved in the transformation and the courage to test our capacity for commitment to sustain such change" (p. 235).

In the section that follows we share six lynchpins that are vital to ensuring that collaborative inquiry reaches scale. We begin by considering Coburn's (2003) redefinition of scale, followed by our observations regarding what educators need to be aware of in order to prevent collaborative inquiry from being adopted superficially. The six lynchpins are meant to be insightful and instructive in regard to redefining the scale of collaborative inquiry and will help leaders to identify and address the conditions needed to bring about a wider and deeper adoption.

COBURN'S (2003) REDEFINITION OF SCALE

In educational research, the term *scale* often refers to how widely spread a reform (usually a novel teaching or instructional practice) is within a district or system. Scale is typically measured by the number of teachers introduced to the reform and, in turn, schools reporting that the innovation has been implemented in classrooms. In response to this widely accepted definition of scale, Coburn (2003) advocated for a more dynamic definition in research. The author argued that the current metric of scale is problematic, because it only measures the reach of a reform, not the depth of change the reform proposes to make. Underscoring the argument for greater depth, Coburn (2003) suggested that classroom practice reforms should ultimately cause teachers to examine their beliefs and assumptions about "how students learn, the nature of subject matter, expectations for students, or what constitutes effective instruction" (p. 4).

The challenges of bringing collaborative inquiry to scale are not inherent in the design itself. Collaborative inquiry, if adopted as intended, is a way to achieve Coburn's (2003) redefined notion of scale. For example, Coburn (2003) argued that "definitions of scale must include attention to the nature of change in classroom instruction; issues of sustainability; spread of norms, principles, and beliefs; and a shift in ownership such that a reform can become self-generative" (p. 3). The collaborative inquiry process brings the nature of change in classroom instruction to the forefront. Change *is* sustainable when it is initiated by teachers—within a supportive professional learning community. Shift in ownership occurs as an internal effort and not an imposed, external reform.

....

Collaborative inquiry, if adopted as intended, is a way to achieve Coburn's (2003) redefined notion of scale.

....

During the process, individuals consider espoused theories in light of theories-in-use. As a result of reconciling the discrepancy between initial thinking and new ideas that emerged through the examination of evidence and reflection, changes in beliefs occur. Numerous statements collected from participants over the years are evidence of such changes in beliefs. A classroom teacher recently noted, "I used to think that it would be difficult to show evidence of my effectiveness as a teacher but now I know that student work is the best way to show my impact." A vice principal recently stated, "Now that I know differently, I could never go back to the way I used to do things."

....

As a result of reconciling the discrepancy between initial thinking and new ideas that emerged through the examination of evidence and reflection, changes in beliefs occur.

....

CONDITIONS NECESSARY TO BRING COLLABORATIVE INQUIRY TO SCALE

While we believe that scale, as redefined by Coburn (2003), is attainable through the utilization of a collaborative inquiry approach to professional

"Beliefs and practices about professional development are shifting. Research is pointing to the relationship between teachers who work together collaboratively and a resulting improvement in student learning" (Hirsh & Killion, 2007, p. 101).

learning, some of the ways in which collaborative inquiry is being carried out directly prevent Coburn's notions of scale from coming to fruition. Based on our work with teams, schools, and districts, we have identified six lynchpins that are vital to ensuring collaborative inquiry will reach a critical mass or tipping point from which its breadth and depth can spread change in thinking and practice throughout school districts. These lynchpins underscore the adaptive challenge in bringing collaborative inquiry to scale and if ill considered can relegate collaborative inquiry to another failed attempt to improve learning for students and teachers.

Lynchpin #1—Voluntary Participation

We have seen collaborative inquiry play out differently in districts across North America. Where we have witnessed greater success (that is a realization of Coburn's notion of scale) is in districts in which educators were *invited* to participate in the process. This invitation sets the stage for trust of and among teachers. It also signals a belief to educators that they are capable of self-directing meaningful and impactful professional learning and confirms for teachers that everyone engaged embraces a *learning for improvement* stance. This invitation acknowledges teachers as professionals and provides for a level of autonomy that is needed to shift ownership of reforms.

Where collaborative inquiry, however, has been introduced as a mandate, educators approach it with skepticism and often associate it with past professional development experiences—which may have been inappropriate to address the daily challenges they face. When educators are forced into the experience, they do not seem to recognize the elements of effective professional learning are inherent in the design. Various forms of resistance (including "this is not the job I signed up for") result when educators are forced to facilitate and/or participate.

Lynchpin #2—Shared Leadership

Collaborative inquiry provides participants with the autonomy to make decisions as they test solutions related to their challenges of practice and formulate answers to the questions set out at the start of the cycle. Formal leaders are required to resist the temptation to solve problems and invest the time needed for others to discover what works best.

When formal leaders provide opportunities for shared leadership by affording others the power to make decisions, everyone benefits.

As a member of a professional learning community in a secondary school a few years ago, one of us witnessed what can be made possible when teachers are entrusted and empowered to lead change. The principal had identified five priorities and formed "action teams" that consisted of teachers (one teacher was assigned as a lead for each team) from various departments within the school. Each action team was responsible for one of the following priorities: planning for school improvement; increasing student voice; improving the school's tutorial program; improving outcomes on the Ontario Secondary School Literacy Test (OSSLT); and overseeing the School Effectiveness Framework (SEF) process. The teams worked both independently and together in order to improve student experiences and achievement. They adopted an inquiry stance, asking questions such as "How can we involve students more meaningfully in school improvement?" and "Who are our students at greatest risk and what can be done to ensure their success?" The teachers engaged in open, honest, and difficult conversations as they grappled with their questions in search of improving student outcomes.

> Copland (2003) conducted an in-depth analysis of patterns of inquiry practices that developed within schools over time. Findings suggested that establishing new leadership structures—for example, a rotating lead teacher—was linked with developing a school culture that supported inquiry-based change. The researcher noted that these opportunities built capacity within the faculty and worked in favor of sustaining the reform. The researcher also noted that "the use of an inquiry process is centrally important to building capacity for school improvement and a vehicle for developing and distributing leadership" (p. 375).

We had witnessed similar approaches to shared leadership in schools before. It is not uncommon, in our experiences, to work alongside administrators who have assembled teams of teachers to lead change initiatives. However, what was different about the principal in this example was that he turned decision-making power over to the teachers. He actively sought their opinions and allowed them to go forward with solutions related to their inquiries, even if he felt they might fail. Teachers were provided the autonomy to make and learn from mistakes. In recalling a discussion with the administrator, one of us questioned a practice one of the action teams was pursuing in relation to their inquiry. Rather than telling the team what to do, he stepped back and quietly monitored, believing that they would come to their own conclusion about the lack of effectiveness in their approach. They quickly did and changed their direction in pursuit of more effective practices. That spring, the school's Ontario Secondary School

"Under conditions of true complexity—where the knowledge required exceeds that of any individual and unpredictability reigns—efforts to dictate every step from the center will fail. People need room to act and adapt" (Gawande, 2009, p. 79).

Derrington and Angelle (2013) found "a clear and strong relationship between collective efficacy and the extent of teacher leadership in a school," (p. 6) noting that "the strong positive relationship between the constructs of teacher leadership and collective efficacy promotes success for students, teachers, and schools" (p. 6).

When district leaders become involved in professional learning through a participatory approach and develop teachers by sharing leadership and providing for collaborative structures, their involvement can foster trust among the stakeholders and aid in the development of a collective efficacy (Horton & Martin, 2013, p. 64).

Literacy Test (OSSLT) results showed a 21 percent increase in the success rate for first-time eligible students and a 19 percent increase in the success rate for previously eligible students. In addition, the gap in achievement between students enrolled in applied courses and students enrolled in academic courses decreased by 21 percent.

Fortunately, it is becoming more common to witness instances where formal administrators stand back and trust the process of teachers innovating together. However, in some places, where formal leaders refer to "shared or distributed leadership," it merely amounts to teachers occupying a seat on a school improvement team, and teachers' roles in decision-making are often tokenized. If collaborative inquiry is going to reach scale, formal leaders need to resist the temptation to solve problems for others. Emihovich and Battaglia (2000) noted "The development of a critical community of equal voice is an exhausting enterprise which demands stamina on the part of the community leader and a strong conviction that qualities such as empowerment, collegiality, diversity, and risk-taking are worth more than certainty, stability, and efficiency. As school leaders, it is often difficult to resist the temptation to deliver information, direct action, solve problems, and offer advice to teachers rather than exert the patience and provide opportunities for these qualities to evolve naturally over time" (p. 235).

Lynchpin #3—Guided From Experience

It is more difficult to guide something if you have not had the opportunity to experience it yourself. You can muddle your way through, but in the end, certain nuances can only be understood through genuine engagement in a process. This is true when it comes to collaborative inquiry. By engaging in the process, leaders not only come to understand, appreciate, and value it as a powerful professional learning design, it also enables richer and deeper conversations between system leaders and other educators. Leaders are better equipped to provide support for those leading collaborative inquiry teams. In addition, when leadership at the system level models what they expect other educators to do, they demonstrate that they truly value and believe in the process.

> Katz et al. (2009) describe activity traps as *"doings* that, while well intentioned, are not truly needs based and have the effect of diverting resources (both human and material) away from where they are most necessary" (p. 24).

A recent conversation with a school principal underscores the importance of system leaders engaging in the process. The principal did not need to be convinced about the transformative power of collaborative inquiry; she had witnessed it in previous years. She had documented evidence that it was improving the culture in her building and impacting student outcomes. What she was struggling with was protecting the time and autonomy of her staff to continue to engage in the process as a new supervisory officer was placing demands

> "Leaders should be doing, and should be seen doing, that which they expect or require others to do. Likewise, leaders should expect to have their own practice subjected to the same scrutiny as they exercise toward others" (Elmore, 2008, p. 67).

on the staff that the principal believed would inevitably lead to activity traps. She did not want to divert time and attention away from what mattered the most—addressing student-learning needs. While the school district was invested in collaborative inquiry as an approach to school improvement, the new supervisory officer did not understand enough about it to trust the process and therefore was interfering in ways that concerned the administrator. While he continued to indicate that he was in support of collaborative inquiry, his expectations often contradicted this support. There was inconsistency between his espoused theory and his theory-in-use.

Addressing Challenges of Leadership Through Collaborative Inquiry

Marty Chaffee, administrator leadership consultant with Oakland Schools, supports administrators in order to build their competence and confidence as school leaders. Marty engages administrator teams in collaborative inquiry in

(Continued)

(Continued)

order to help them deal with the challenges of leadership practice related to feedback and coaching, growing a staff culture, and improving instruction. Principal and participant Patricia Chinn noted that working through the collaborative inquiry process and being able to study the process with colleagues has given her the opportunity to focus her efforts and to really understand and evaluate her impact on leading change. Patricia noted that "Having been a part of this process myself and seeing how to pose an inquiry question, develop theories of action, gather all forms of data, and come together to discuss results makes me extremely excited to engage in the process with my team." Jim Lalik, also a principal in Oakland County, has learned that discovering that something does not have the impact expected by the team is great information. He also noted that what he is learning about leadership is that he doesn't have to know it all. Jim also felt that a focused theory of action keeps the team grounded during the journey.

In a study by Emihovich and Battaglia (2000) that sought to determine aspects of the school leadership role that needed to change in order to be successful in promoting collaborative inquiry, the researchers concluded school leaders needed to do more than support teachers' efforts in reconceptualizing practice. The authors noted that school leaders needed to become "authentic learners and integral players in the learning environments they endeavour to create" (p. 233). Furthermore, the researchers suggested that school leaders become participant learners by "inquiring, studying, reading, writing, analyzing, questioning, and contributing to the collective understanding" (p. 234). As stated earlier, Coburn (2003) suggested that classroom practice reforms should ultimately cause teachers to examine their beliefs and assumptions about "how students learn, the nature of subject matter, expectations for students, or what constitutes effective instruction" (p. 4). Collaborative inquiry, when engaged in at a system level, causes leaders to examine beliefs and assumptions about how teachers learn, the nature of professional learning, expectations for educators, and what constitutes effective leadership. In school districts where system leaders engage in collaborative inquiry and reflect on the incongruence between theories-in-use and theories espoused, systemic change is more likely to be realized and sustained. When system leaders guide from experience, change is more easily accomplished.

"Inquiry is difficult for individual teachers to do in isolation from their colleagues or from leaders. Nor can leaders decide what the focus of their inquiry should be. It is the collaborative inquiry process that matters" (Timperley et al., 2014, p. 5).

Lynchpin #4—Achieved Coherence

The fourth lynchpin involves balancing the tension between district-driven improvement and classroom-driven improvement. It speaks to aligning the focus of teacher's inquiries and the goals identified in district and school improvement plans. Quinn (2015) noted, however, that alignment alone is not sufficient and described achieving coherence as "connecting the mindsets of everyone that need to be engaged in moving things forward" (p. 6). Quinn (2015) noted that what is needed is "people who are in a continuous process of making and remaking meaning by doing the work and doing it together" (p. 7). This lynchpin brings to light the following questions: How are the learning needs in district improvement plans (or school improvement plans) and the learning needs identified by collaborative inquiry teams similar and/or different? Which should inform the other? How are collaborative inquiry teams and school improvement teams working together? We wonder how the complementary nature of these two processes could be capitalized upon.

> Bushe and Marshak (2015) noted that "the resulting processes of participative inquiry, engagement, and reflection are designed to maximize diversity, surface the variety of perspectives and motivations without privileging any one, and allow convergences and coherence to emerge" (p. 18).

In school districts where we support teacher-driven improvement, collaborative inquiry cycles and school improvement planning are often viewed as two distinct processes. One difference is based on the types of evidence examined when identifying learning needs. Trailing data, including standardized test scores and cohort data, often inform district and school-based plans. Evidence obtained through observations, conversations, and student work products garnered from the students that sit in front of educators every day is the source driving collaborative inquiries. Both are important. Where the difficulty lies is when the district identifies a focus—for example, improving outcomes in mathematics—and the majority of collaborative inquiry teams have identified student-learning needs rooted in literacy. System goals and teachers' goals are disconnected, and as a result, the inquiries do not deliver on the district's improvement plans.

For collaborative inquiry to reach scale, teachers need to see that it is not another initiative; it is their important contribution to school

> "When central office staff relinquishes to school-based leaders key decisions about a school's goals and the pathway to achieving those goals, interventions are often more focused on the unique nature of the school and its students and staff. When teachers' voices shape the nature of professional learning, their learning is deeply connected to their classroom work, students' learning needs, and the curriculum they teach" (Hirsh & Killion, 2007, p. 39).

improvement. However, in districts where the two processes are incoherent, system-wide professional learning days are usually devoted to topics prioritized and determined by central office staff and therefore disconnected from the learning related to the inquiry. Teachers come to believe their collaborative inquiry work is an add-on. In districts where collaborative inquiry teams are provided time during system-wide professional learning days to engage in the cycle (rather than learn about something else), they come to see that their work is directly related to the school improvement planning process. Coherence is achieved through the process of shared and continuous improvement.

....

For collaborative inquiry to reach scale, teachers need to see that it is not another initiative; it is their important contribution to school improvement.

....

In order for collaborative inquiry to reach scale, systems need to achieve coherence between the goals and strategies articulated in larger improvement efforts and those articulated in teacher initiated change. We need to capitalize on the complementary relationship between collaborative inquiry cycles and school improvement planning rather than treating them as two distinct processes. Additionally, systems would benefit from determining how to align the time allocated for professional learning with the work of collaborative inquiry teams.

Johnson (2012) found that teachers who were provided with daily time to collaborate on instructional issues had a greater perception of collective efficacy than those who were not provided daily collaboration time. The researcher noted, "There is a significant difference in the mean level of collective teacher efficacy between teachers provided with scheduled time during the day to collaborate instructionally versus those who are not" (p. 68).

Lynchpin #5—Learning Is Recognized and Disseminated

Good ideas spread exponentially throughout a system once a tipping point is reached. This tipping point is described by Gladwell (2002) as "a place where the unexpected becomes expected, where radical change is more than possibility" (p. 13). Since collaborative inquiry has potential to fundamentally change the way teachers engage in ongoing professional learning, it requires strong groups of advocates to share the positive impact it has had on their understanding of professional collaboration to improve student learning. We have noticed that when districts and schools do not put in place mechanisms for this sharing to take place then opportunities for collaborative inquiry to spread are limited. We have witnessed diminished enthusiasm for collaborative inquiry when teachers perceive that the reach of their learning is limited to their classrooms only. Rather than provide the impetus needed for collaborative inquiry to reach a tipping point, schools and districts inadvertently create disillusionment with the process.

One of us recently returned to a school district to work with teacher leaders who volunteered to facilitate peers through a collaborative inquiry cycle. This was the third year in which teacher-led collaborative inquiry was supported by the school district. One participant who had skillfully assisted teams in previous years spoke about what his team had learned about identifying First Nations, Métis, and Inuit student learning needs and increasing student success. They had conducted substantial reviews of literature, tried and tested new teaching approaches in their own environment, and talked to students at length to obtain greater insight. They wrote a report after each cycle, as they recognized the importance in documenting the learning. Unfortunately, the administration had failed to acknowledge not only the team's efforts but also neglected to read the report. The teacher leader expressed the following concern: "I believe in this process. Last year our group made great gains and we wrote a substantial report. What I worry about is that the report is shelved and it is gathering dust."

Even though everyone would like their efforts acknowledged, this participant was more concerned with disseminating the knowledge their team created so that other educators could learn from it and students could benefit. As previously discussed, collaborative inquiry honors the professionalism of teachers as they build their knowledge to improve student learning. Some teachers have become disenfranchised with education because their voice in school improvement efforts go largely unheard. If schools and districts are unable to provide platforms for teachers to share their learning from collaborative inquiry, then a tremendous opportunity to engage teachers as partners in spreading and deepening school improvement efforts is missed.

Lynchpin #6—Skilled Facilitation

A final lynchpin critical to scaling collaborative inquiry is skilled facilitation. While collaborative inquiry is initiated, shaped, and driven by teachers, it must be guided by skilled teacher facilitators. Since collaborative inquiry is a process that surfaces the beliefs and assumptions underlying current teaching practices to propose and attempt new approaches, a skilled facilitator is critical in ensuring that the process is faithful to its intended outcome. To reach this outcome, a facilitator must be able to support a team in three ways. First, the facilitator must help teams establish

> Situations that cannot be adequately addressed within the context of an organization's current beliefs and values "often require the leader to orchestrate conflict to facilitate the evolution of new beliefs and values that allow for actions not possible within the context of the old system" (Marzano, Waters, & McNulty, 2005, p. 23).

and maintain a needs-based focus. Second, the facilitator must be able to provoke the thinking necessary for educators to critically analyze the impact their inquiry has on student learning. This includes helping team members reconcile discrepancies between espoused theories and theories-in-use. Third, facilitators must mindfully shape the development of a professional learning culture. Depth results when facilitators are able to support teams in these ways, and therefore, the conditions needed for spread and sustainability are more likely to be achieved.

However, when facilitators are less skilled at helping teams uncover student and educator learning needs, provoking thinking, reconciling discrepancies in theories, and shaping the development of a professional learning culture, collaborative inquiry can be experienced as a rigid lock-step process. Participants go through the motions; ticking off each phase as if it is a checklist of activities to perform. In the end, teachers are unable to articulate the positive impact collaborative inquiry has had on both their professional learning and the learning of students. As a result, school and district leaders are further challenged to ensure that the resources and processes needed to bring collaborative inquiry to scale are in place.

A study by Nelson (2008) demonstrated the importance of the role of facilitator. In examining the transformative potential of collaborative inquiry, the actions of three different facilitators resulted in different trajectories for their teams. As one team abandoned the inquiry cycle, collective activities shifted from inquiry to curriculum alignment and dialogue predominately focused on collectively planning and implementing lessons. Subsequent to determining the inquiry focus, the team did not examine classroom data to understand learners nor to inform decisions. Nelson (2008) noted that the team had little support from a facilitator, therefore lacking a critical other, who might have posed questions that teachers were not raising. The researcher noted that in the absence of the facilitator there was no one to guide the team "toward an inquiry stance, where they might pose questions that would help them examine the impact of these new lessons on the diverse students in their classrooms" (p. 564).

> "For collaboration to be an enabler of the kind of meaningful professional learning that can impact on practice, it needs to be more than just an inventory of group-based activities that we hope will make a difference" (Katz et al., 2009, p. 45).

The second collaborative inquiry team in the Nelson (2008) study was focused on increasing students' command of mathematical and scientific language in order to increase student achievement. The team reported trying "something at each phase of the inquiry cycle" (p. 564). This team had a facilitator who helped them stay focused and provided access to protocols and relevant research literature. However, a "culture of niceness" seemed to inhibit the team's "willingness or abilities to question each other's stated beliefs" (p. 567). Even the questions posed by the facilitator dealt with keeping the team focused on the agenda rather than probing to help team members in challenging ideas. Most importantly, teachers did not develop common strategies for teaching students about scientific investigations or experiments—as reported by one team member, "we didn't change strategies throughout the year; we've just kept our same strategies" (p. 568).

The third collaborative inquiry team in the Nelson (2008) study, however, was led by a skilled facilitator. The team began with the inquiry question, "How can we increase student use of evidence and inferential logic in constructing scientific explanations?" This team not only completed the inquiry cycle, they made recursive loops back through different phases and, based on the instructional changes made, collectively analyzed classroom data multiple times in relation to student learning. The team narrowed their inquiry question to focus specifically on scientific conclusions. The facilitator ensured student-learning evidence was examined multiple times and helped to focus dialogue on the impact of the team's actions on student learning as well as what to do about their still existing questions.

As demonstrated in the study by Nelson (2008), a skilled facilitator will help to foster and sustain a culture of collaborative inquiry by surfacing and negotiating discrepancies in beliefs, maintaining norms and agreed upon avenues for dialogue, employing protocols when necessary, and focusing the team on relevant evidence. For these reasons, a skilled facilitator is vital to the team as they engage in a cycle of inquiry.

Collaborative inquiry is poised to transform professional learning from the inside out. It transforms educators' thinking about learning, leading, and teaching to ultimately inform and change their practices. Collaborative inquiry embodies what the research supports as a viable way to create self-sustaining improvement processes that are teacher directed. In the first part of this book, we have described the transformative potential of collaborative inquiry. We have also described the conditions for its transformative power to spread throughout schools and districts. The challenge therefore remains in ensuring that what is spread is not only deep and wide but relevant and meaningful to educators engaged in collaborative inquiry. To meet this challenge, knowledge and skills regarding aspects of the inquiry process need to be strengthened.

In the second part of this book, we highlight these aspects in relation to the collaborative inquiry framework described in Chapter 1. Beginning with determining a needs-based focus, the following ideas are explored: (a) what constitutes a needs-based focus; (b) formulating meaningful inquiry questions; and (c) developing robust theories of action. When provoking thinking to assess impact, questions to consider when collecting data are offered along with ideas to build appreciation for and capacity to use a variety of assessment data. Strategies for engaging teams in collaborative analysis of student work are shared. In addition, ways to close the gap between theories of action (espoused theories versus theories-in-use) are considered. Finally, in shaping the development of a professional learning culture, the following ideas are explored: shifting from professional development to professional learning, building quality professional relationships, improving collaboration, and expanding the reach of learning.

Part II

Strengthening the Power

Realizing Change in Schools and Classrooms

3 Determining and Maintaining a Focus

"Laser-like professional learning focused on improving student learning produces deep change" (Hirsh & Killion, 2007, p. 64).

Figure 3.1 Determining and Maintaining a Focus

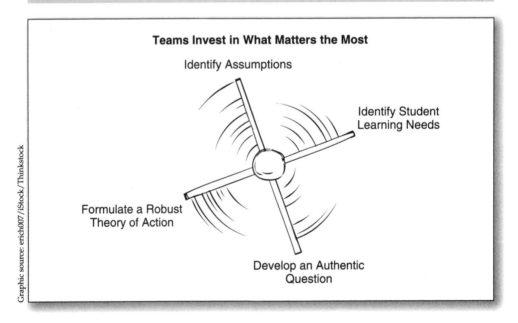

Graphic source: erich007/iStock/Thinkstock

During the first stage in the collaborative inquiry cycle, teams determine a focus for their inquiry. There is general consensus that a focus, based on the learning needs of students, will help in steering teams toward the desired result of improving student outcomes. In our work, however, we have found that educators hold very different ideas of what constitutes a student-learning need. People define *learning needs* in different ways. In addition, we have observed that inquiry questions are sometimes formulaic and driven by factors other than participants' *need to know*. Finally, reasons behind the development of a theory of action are often misunderstood, and therefore theories lose their potential to engage educators in the deep reflection required to bring about conceptual change. Therefore, in order to strengthen the collaborative inquiry process, it is important to develop a common understanding of student-learning needs, fine-tune the criteria related to developing a strong inquiry question, and heighten awareness behind the purposes served by articulating a theory of action. Suggestions for strengthening this stage in the process are outlined below.

> "Absent a clear notion of what constitutes the important problems for focus, leadership work can become dissipated and undirected" (Copland, 2003, p. 379).

ESTABLISHING A NEEDS-BASED FOCUS

As the collaborative inquiry process unfolds, one of the first steps is for teams to identify a focus for their work. As noted by Reeves (2010) "the pursuit of high-impact learning requires not only that we achieve individual and organizational focus, but also that we focus on the right things" (p. 65). The team's inquiry is driven by a central question, composed by team members, that identifies a challenge they are experiencing related to learning, leading, and/or teaching. Timperley et al. (2014) pointed out that focusing requires us to ask "Where are we going to concentrate our energies so that we can change the experiences and outcomes for our learners?" (p. 10). In establishing a focus, Katz et al. (2009) noted that "the goal is to identify the most urgent student learning needs" (p. 29).

> As previously stated, scaling collaborative inquiry to the point where the entire organization is transformed requires that a learning stance is assumed and maintained at all levels in the system. While the goal of a collaborative inquiry team comprised of teachers is to identify *student*-learning needs, a team comprised of school-based administrators' goal is to identify the most urgent *teacher*-learning needs. System-based administrators' goals would focus on *school-based administrators*' learning needs and so on. While teachers' learning will be related to teaching practices, school and system leaders' learning will more likely be focused on the practice of leadership.

The problem is not gaining consensus that a collaborative team's focus should be on student-learning needs. Teams readily agree that addressing student-learning needs *is* the priority. The problem is that educators have very different ideas about what constitutes a student-learning need. As a result, helping a team to identify a needs-based focus is not always a simple task for facilitators.

Our experiences working with a variety of educators—including elementary and secondary teachers, coaches, administrators, superintendents, and directors—confirms the notion that educators define student *learning* very differently. Consider the following statements:

1. Students need wait time and effective questioning to prompt their thinking.

2. Students need opportunities to see the teacher and other students thinking aloud as they work through problem solving.

3. Students need explicit instruction using a gradual release of responsibility.

While we agree with each of the above statements, we argue that they do not identify a student-*learning* need. Hattie and Yates (2014) noted that the theme of learning is often absent in educational conversations, which tend to focus more on teaching than they do on *learning*. Katz and Dack (2013) noted that practitioners tend to engage "with the concept of focus through the dominant culture of activity, rather than an alternative culture of learning" (p. 39) and that focus is often "interpreted as a teaching focus, not a learning focus" (p. 39). Statements 1, 2, and 3 identify how a peer or teacher might *respond* to a student-learning need (note the focus on *teaching* rather than *learning*). While identifying student-learning needs, we need to ensure that we do not get caught in what Katz et al. (2009) refer to as "activity traps" (p. 24) by formulating a solution prior to identifying the real problem.

In addition to identifying a *teaching* focus rather than a *learning* focus, beginning teams sometimes identify a *behavioral* focus rather than a *learning* focus. Consider the following:

1. Students need to show respect for themselves, their classmates, and their teachers.

2. Students need to come to class prepared.

> 3. Students need to stop using devices when the teacher is teaching. They need to know when it is appropriate to use devices in the classroom and when they should be turned off and stored.

These statements identify desirable student behaviors that teachers hope to foster and see flourish in their students but do not necessitate a collaborative inquiry in order to address. Not every professional dilemma requires that teams engage in a collaborative inquiry cycle in order for the dilemma to be solved (Katz, personal communication, August 21, 2013). When teams begin to consider a needs-based focus for their inquiries, it is not uncommon to hear statements like the ones listed above. As the first stage of the collaborative inquiry process unfolds, facilitators must help team members construct common understandings of student-learning needs.

What does constitute a student-*learning* need? Student-learning needs stem from issues that are *affective*, *cognitive*, or *metacognitive* in nature. Affective needs focus on emotional growth and include self-confidence, interpersonal skills, enthusiasm for learning, and intrinsic motivation. Cognitive-learning needs focus on internal mental processes used to make meaning, including summarizing and synthesizing, inferring, activating prior knowledge, evaluating, comparing and contrasting, the skill of argumentation, and so forth. Finally, metacognitive needs focus on planning, monitoring, and evaluating one's own cognition. While the needs identified will be uniquely situated within each discipline, focusing on *learning* provides a common starting point.

Affective Student-Learning Needs

Affective needs are rooted in emotions, feelings, and attitudes that influence learning. Think of a time when you may have experienced one or more of the following emotions and/or attitudes in relation to learning. What impact did these emotions or attitudes have on your learning experience?

> Timperley et al. (2014) offered an updated and revised spiral of inquiry framework for transforming learning in schools. Noting that "one of the most important differences in this new framework is the involvement of learners" (p. 5), the authors recommended that collaborative inquiry teams include students in identifying and addressing issues in their learning environment. The examples of inquiry questions focusing on affective, cognitive, and metacognitive student-learning needs provided here are purposely phrased with student participation in mind. Note that based on the wording of each example, teachers and students could be pursuing the inquiry in partnership.

Emotions and Attitudes That Impact Learning

anxiety	indifference
cynicism	negativity
embarrassment	overwhelmed
fear	resentment
frustration	stress
impatience	

There is no doubt that learning is interrupted when negative emotions and attitudes surface, as such feelings hinder our ability to make sense of things. Sylwester (1994) noted that emotion "drives attention, which in turn drives learning and memory" (p. 60). Darling-Hammond, Orcutt, Strobel, Kirsch, Lit, and Martin (n.d.) pointed out that "emotions can interfere with students' learning in several ways; including (1) limiting the capacity to balance emotional issues with schoolwork, (2) creating anxiety specifically about schoolwork, and (3) triggering emotional responses to classroom events" (p. 90). Many of the negative emotions listed above cause stress. Tough (2012) provided evidence that stress compromises executive functioning abilities. Finally, Stein and Book (2006) argued that "in order for us to take advantage and flex our cognitive intelligence to the maximum, we first need good emotional intelligence" (p. 5). There is general consensus in the educational community and numerous studies that provide evidence that learning is influenced by emotion.

Competency Beliefs

I can succeed.

I am not very smart.

I really suck at math.

I am capable of achieving.

I can reach my goals.

I can't do this work. It is beyond me.

I am good at solving problems.

I'll never figure this out.

What is the adaptive challenge related to student-learning needs embedded in emotions? Sylwester (1994) suggested that "because we don't fully understand our emotional system, we don't know exactly how to regulate it in school, beyond defining too much or too little emotion as misbehavior" (p. 60). The author also suggested that the teaching profession has not "fully addressed the important relationship between a stimulating and emotionally positive classroom experience and the overall health of both students and staff" (p. 60). If a collaborative inquiry team relates with Sylwester's assertions and has identified negative emotions or attitudes as a student-learning need that seems to be getting in the way of student success, then the dilemma would be an adaptive challenge for that particular team.

Affective needs are also manifested in students' motivations, competency beliefs, and attributions for success and failure, which steer future expectations for learning. Zumbrunn, Tadlock, and Roberts (2011) noted that "intrinsic motivation and volition guide the level of effort and persistence" (p. 8) students use when completing assignments. Motivation is closely linked to competency beliefs and attributions. If students believe that they can successfully accomplish a particular task, they are more likely to select challenging tasks, stay with them longer, and perform better. In addition, when students attribute success to effort and strategy use, they start using better strategies (Dweck, 2006). Tough (2012) suggested that "in the last few years, economists, educators, psychologists, and neuroscientists have begun to produce evidence that developing non-cognitive skills such as persistence, self-control, curiosity, conscientiousness, grit, and self-confidence" (p. xv) is what matters most. Understanding the scientific research on human motivation including strategies for self-regulating motivation would be very beneficial for educators. By understanding the role of competency beliefs and attributions for success and failure, collaborative inquiry teams would be able to help students develop attitudes and beliefs that facilitate motivation and performance.

Motivating all students is not a simple task for educators. Many classrooms utilize extrinsic reward systems, providing stickers, candy, free

Success Attributions

I was successful, because the task was really easy.

I was able to do well, because I worked hard and studied the right material.

I didn't do well, because the questions on the test were unfair. The teacher tried to trick the class.

I nailed it! The strategies I used really helped.

All my studying paid off.

I didn't quite meet the mark. I'll need to concentrate harder and select better strategies next time.

There were too many distractions. I could not concentrate.

I didn't study very hard.

Physics is difficult because I am a girl.

I could have done better, if I had focused my attention during class time.

If the teacher had given me more time, I would have done better.

time, and longer recesses in exchange for work completion, good behavior, and good grades. Pink (2009) cited multiple studies and examples that call into question the conventional view of human motivation and noted the "counterintuitive consequences of extrinsic incentives" (p. 37). Hattie (2012) noted that extrinsic rewards lead to "greater shallow learning of surface features and completion of the work regardless of the standard and for the sake of praise or similar rewards" (p. 42). Pink (2009) argued that "intrinsic motivation—the drive to do something because it is interesting, challenging, and absorbing" (p. 46) is the "strongest and most pervasive driver [of learning]" (p. 23). Figuring out the right balance between extrinsic and intrinsic rewards and designing tasks that motivate each and every student is an adaptive challenge for our educational system. Tackling this adaptive challenge will likely require new learning, along with a shift in beliefs and practice, and therefore it is a focus suitable for a collaborative inquiry team.

Figuring out the right balance between extrinsic and intrinsic rewards and designing tasks that motivate each and every student is an adaptive challenge for our educational system. Tackling this adaptive challenge will likely require new learning, along with a shift in beliefs and practice, and therefore it is a focus suitable for a collaborative inquiry team.

Examples of Inquiry Questions That Delve Into Affective Student-Learning Needs Include the Following:

How can emotions that impede learning be managed inside and outside the classroom?

How can internal motivation to complete tasks be nurtured?

What can be done to shift mindsets from fixed to growth?

How can a sense of belonging be fostered in the classroom?

How might feedback be structured to encourage resilience and perseverance?

How can work tasks be designed to build cooperative relationships between students?

What types of classroom motivators encourage engagement and commitment to learning?

Cognitive Student-Learning Needs

Cognition is the process of acquiring knowledge and involves how individuals interact with information to reorganize and expand knowledge and develop conceptual frameworks. Cognitive-learning needs have to do with the principles of information processing. Our minds process and retain information through the use of different cognitive strategies that include elaboration strategies (e.g., metaphors, mnemonic devices, predicting, paraphrasing, analogies, etc.), organizational strategies (e.g., concept maps, graphic organizers, note making, etc.), memory or recall strategies (e.g., chunking, rehearsal, repetition, etc.), orienting strategies (e.g., skim and scan, using text features, activating prior knowledge, establishing purpose, etc.), and comprehension strategies (e.g., questioning, summarizing, inferring, etc.) to name a few.

All students benefit from cognitive strategy instruction. In order to be independent, self-directed learners, students need a wide variety of cognitive strategies, which will require explicit instruction and practice. In Hattie and Yates' (2014) review of the processes that underpin learning, the authors noted that "one of the most important developments to emerge from research into human learning in recent years is known under the general label of cognitive load" (p. 146). The authors suggested that in order to help students learn, a variety of instructional procedures can be employed in order to reduce the cognitive load. Wood, Woloshyn, and Willoughby (1995) also identified and explained the "array of cognitive strategies which help students to actively organize the information they are expected to learn" (p. 2) and describe the relationship between cognitive effort and more sophisticated and less sophisticated strategies. Hattie and Yates (2014) noted the importance of teachers becoming "more effective when they begin to see the learning process through the eyes of their students" (p. xiii) and listed cognitive load theory as providing teachers with a "means of attempting to view the world through the eyes of a student" (p. 153).

Might issues related to cognitive-learning needs be an adaptive challenge for some educators? Hattie and Yates (2014) stated that "many of those involved in our profession would struggle to name two competing learning theories, let alone defend a notion of learning (and by this we do not mean defending activities that students 'do' but how they learn)" (p. xi). The authors cited reasons for this, including the decline of educational psychology in preservice teacher programs, an emphasis on assessment and curriculum, and the lack of debate about models of learning in literature.

In addition, many teachers (especially secondary school teachers) tend to view themselves as content area experts and do not fully understand their role in developing these types of skills in students. Perhaps this is because they fail to see the relevance to their subject matter or feel discredited. Often, content area teachers have not been trained in cognitive strategy instruction and therefore do not feel equipped to address it. Hattie (2012) noted that "the act of teaching requires deliberate interventions to ensure that there is cognitive change in the student" (p. 16) and suggested that teachers "focus on students' cognitive engagement with the content of what it is that is being taught" (p. 19). This might require a complete reconstruction of existing practice on the part of some teachers, and therefore, the idea of embedded strategy instruction will be an adaptive challenge for some.

Examples of Inquiry Questions That Delve Into Cognitive Student-Learning Needs Include the Following:

What is happening (cognitively) during *each stage of the writing process*?

(Note: substitute *inquiry*, *problem-solving*, or *each step of the scientific method*, etc.)

What makes deep-learning experiences different from others?

What strategies work best for deep learning versus surface learning?

What are the cognitive demands within this subject (or task), and which strategies match these demands?

What strategies can be employed to increase working memory?

What factors inhibit or increase retention?

Metacognitive Student-Learning Needs

As noted above, the key to successful learning lies in a learner's knowledge of various strategies, how they can be used, and when and why to employ them. Success also depends on the self-regulatory skills of planning, monitoring, and evaluating learning. Metacognitive awareness encompasses two these components: (1) knowledge of cognition and (2) regulation of cognition.

Knowledge of cognition refers to what learners know and understand about the way they learn. It includes declarative knowledge about the factors that influence performance (e.g., knowing one's capacity limitations). It includes procedural knowledge about how to execute different procedures (e.g., how to chunk and categorize new information). And finally, it includes conditional knowledge about when and why to apply various cognitive strategies (e.g., knowing when and why to create or use a mnemonic device) (Schraw & Moshman, 1995).

Regulation of cognition refers to how well learners can regulate and therefore have the ability to adjust or correct their learning. These sets of activities include planning (e.g., allocating appropriate amounts of time and resources to learning). It also includes monitoring one's comprehension and task performance (e.g., engaging in self-testing). And finally, it includes evaluating (e.g., appraising products and outcomes of one's learning) (Schraw & Moshman, 1995).

Metacognition is a trait that distinguishes expert from novice learners (Bransford, Brown, and Cocking, 2000). Students who are metacognitive are able to consciously focus attention on important information, accurately judge how well they understand something, use intellectual strengths to compensate for weaknesses, and employ fix-up strategies to correct errors. Most importantly, they are their own best self-assessors; this is what is referred to as assessment *as* learning.

Unfortunately, not all students possess these traits. Many do not create plans for approaching learning tasks, struggle when they get confused, and are unaware of the purposes strategies serve in learning. Therefore, there is a need to help students know themselves as learners, be able to recognize when they have or have not acquired sufficient understanding, identify what needs improving and how to improve it, and reflect on the efficiency of the processes and strategies used. Teachers can help students develop self-regulation as a "powerful mechanism for improving learning" (Hattie, 2012, p. 161). Thinking about thinking is a novel concept to some learners. Educators can help students become more metacognitive—learning how to learn can be taught.

Is this an adaptive challenge that a collaborative inquiry team might select as its focus? As metacognition is not directly observable, many consider it an unclear concept. In addition, Lin, Schwartz, and Hatano (2005) argued "conventional applications of metacognition fall short when it comes to the challenges teachers often face" (p. 245). The authors pointed out that the unique qualities of teaching differentiate it from many of the tasks that metacognitive interventions have supported and that "problems encountered in teaching can require days if not months to resolve" (p. 245). The authors also note that good solutions are dependent on "clarifying and reconciling competing values, for example, those of the teachers, the school district, and the students" (p. 245). Teaching for metacognitive awareness might be an adaptive challenge for teams, as it will likely require teachers to reexamine classroom priorities. If content and curriculum coverage is privileged, then valuing the idea of fostering metacognitive habits of mind is likely to conflict with prevailing values and norms. It may also require the acquisition of new knowledge, skills, resources, and tools. Additionally, students may resist, as they have become comfortable with existing practices and experience various concerns when teachers begin to teach differently.

Examples of Inquiry Questions That Delve Into Metacognitive Student-Learning Needs Include the Following:

How can a shared understanding of what makes a good learner be developed?

What can be done when understanding breaks down?

How can mistakes be turned into opportunities for learning?

In what ways is understanding monitored and adjusted?

How can we ensure that everyone can articulate what they are learning and why?

As mentioned earlier, the phrase *student-learning needs* is open to interpretation, and therefore, helping a team to identify a needs-based focus is not always a simple task for facilitators. However, in order to succeed in improving student learning, collaborative inquiry teams must stay focused on the learning needs of students. Spending the time necessary to ensure that team members share a common understanding of student-learning needs is a critical part of the process. Identifying needs that are affective, cognitive, or metacognitive in nature will ensure the work is purposeful and impactful.

Considerations Regarding Multidisciplinary Teams

As pointed out by Timperley et al. (2014), focus is about "identifying a common area many people can buy into and not about everyone choosing her/his own area of interest" (p. 11). A layer of complexity is added for facilitators when collaborative inquiry teams are comprised of teachers from multiple subject areas. Determining a common area of focus is sometimes confounded by the fact that teachers come from different subject areas. This is partially because of the fact that approaches to learning differ among the disciplines (Shanahan & Shanahan, 2008). Heller and Greenleaf (2007) argued that the context of the materials matters greatly and that every content area has its own set of characteristic literacy practices. "All teachers, in every discipline, have reasons to emphasize certain kinds of reading and writing over others, depending on the nature of specific content and skills they want their students to learn" (p. 11). Educators want students to gain essential understandings and develop the ability to effectively utilize the thinking processes that support effective learning in their subject area, and because these processes differ within each discipline, determining a common area of focus may be a bigger challenge when collaborative inquiry teams are cross curricular.

A research study by Little (2002) demonstrated that opportunities for teacher learning and influences on teacher practice were more prevalent when learning communities were organized at a department level, as opposed to teams that were comprised of interdisciplinary teachers. Little (2002) noted that "students' struggles were situated in academic disciplines in important ways that became evident as teachers talked with us and with one another about student performance" (p. 702) and that interdisciplinary teams "lost opportunities to inquire into problems of student success and failure" (p. 702) because of the relative inattention to subject-related issues of learning and teaching.

Researchers Gallimore et al. (2009) reached a similar conclusion in their study of teachers utilizing a collaborative inquiry approach to improving student outcomes. Participants' attributions of improved student performance shifted from external causes to teaching. The researchers believed this shift occurred because of the team's ability to focus on a problem of practice long enough to develop instructional solutions. Seeing causal connections fostered acquisition of key teaching skills and knowledge, such as identifying student needs, formulating instructional plans, and using evidence to refine instruction. The researchers noted that these outcomes were more likely when teams taught similar content, were led by a trained peer-facilitator using an inquiry-focused protocol, and had stable settings in which to engage in continuous improvement.

Grounding learning conversations within the context of the specific disciplines is important to the success of collaborative inquiry teams, as demonstrated by the research cited above. We need to acknowledge that disciplinary experts approach learning in different ways when considering the composition of collaborative inquiry teams. Since stakes are high and a lot is being invested, schools and districts might benefit from rethinking cross-curricular team compositions.

FORMULATING AN INQUIRY QUESTION

"The formulation of powerful questions is at the heart of productive inquiry" (Walsh & Sattes, 2010. p. 4).

Inquiry questions are sometimes formulaic and/or driven by factors other than participants' need to know. In cases where they are formulaic, it is usually because participant involvement has been mandated. Participants follow a formula rather than engaging in inquiries in an authentic way. In other cases, questions are driven by other motivational factors. Recently we came across a teacher librarian who was pursuing an inquiry (she already knew the answer to) in order to secure additional funding for library books. She felt that her principal would provide her with additional funding to purchase a book series if she could demonstrate how that series could boost boys' interest in reading. In another example, a resource teacher was pursuing an inquiry (again he already knew the answer) that related to increasing student achievement through the use of assistive technology. The motive behind his inquiry was to get homeroom teachers to provide access to assistive devices in their classrooms. In both cases, the inquiries were not driven by an authentic question but other motivational factors.

••

Questions posed by collaborative inquiry teams need to come from a place of authenticity, where participants are grappling with issues in which the solution is unknown.

••

As mentioned earlier, sometimes senior administrators determine the question for teams. In one example, a senior administrator offered class sets of iPads as an incentive for teams to inquire about how the iPads could increase mathematics results. While there is good intention in each of these cases, these examples demonstrate how collaborative inquiry can be reduced from a powerful and transformative professional learning opportunity to a means to an end. Questions posed by collaborative inquiry teams need to come from a place of authenticity, where *participants* are grappling with issues in which the solution is unknown. It might stem from a problem of practice that keeps them up at night.

DEVELOPING A ROBUST THEORY OF ACTION

When collaborative inquiry teams articulate a theory of action, it helps to ensure the team's vision is clear to all stakeholders, which will increase the likelihood of success. It also helps to expose their thinking and reasons behind the actions they plan to take. In addition, it will enable the team to reflect on espoused theories and theories-in-use. If discrepancies in thinking are exposed, it will aid in the reconciliation of these discrepancies. New insights are gained through this process, and *learning*, defined by Katz and Dack (2013) as "a permanent change in thinking and behavior" (p. vii), occurs.

A theory of action outlines a sequence of strategic actions that articulate what City, Elmore, Fiarman, and Teitel (2009) referred to as a "storyline that makes a vision and a strategy concrete" (p. 40). A theory of action "puts into words the steps and contingencies that have to be mastered in order for a broad vision or strategy to result in concrete action that influences student learning" (City et al., 2009, p. 44). Fullan (2008) said "the best theories are at their core solidly grounded in action" (p. 1). Bushe (2010) noted that "every goal-oriented action you take is based on some theory you

> A skilled facilitator will ensure that teams develop a question that meets the following criteria:
>
> - Something they are interested in and genuinely curious about
> - Open ended (avoiding yes/no answers)
> - Reasonable (time management and within the team's scope of control)
> - Connected to an urgent-learning need within their classroom/ department/school
> - Requires an answer that is sought through changes in adult actions
> - Not too broad

have about how that action will lead to that goal" (p. 130) and suggested that "if we are trying to accomplish a goal together, it's helpful to be operating from a common theory of action" (p. 131). Therefore, when considering a theory of action in relation to collaborative inquiry, one purpose it serves is to remove the ambiguity from the team's vision of change. Sparks (2007) suggested that when we "develop and communicate clear, coherent, and compelling theories of action through stories and other means" (p. 37), we are more likely to produce the desired results.

A theory of action consists of a sequence of "if/then" statements that illustrate the causality between actions and expected outcomes. Framing theories in the form of a hypothesis (if/then) compels educators to consider causes (instructional and/or leadership practices) that precede effects (student learning/teacher learning/leadership learning). It helps to uncover relationships between teaching and learning and/or leading and change as collaborative inquiry teams examine what they think will work against the realities of what is actually happening given their existing culture, specific context, and unique population. Sparks (2007) suggested that a theory of action "lays out for examination each of the links in a chain of causal events and the underlying assumptions that support them" (p. 38).

Fullan (2008) noted that "good theories are critical because they give you a handle on the underlying reason (really the underlying thinking) behind actions and their consequences" (p. 16). Therefore, a second purpose a theory of action serves is related to reflection and experimentation.

As teams test their theory, they engage in frequent reflection based on their actions and resulting outcomes. In this sense, the experimentation aspect of a theory of action is not in the tradition of a rigorous experimental design or methodology. The intent is not to control for variables in an effort to "prove" causality through statistical analysis. The intent is for educators to evaluate the impact of their actions based on what occurred as a result and then to compare the resulting outcomes to what they initially thought might happen. Initial hunches may be confirmed based on observations and an examination of the evidence. However, if initial thinking is challenged, educators must reconcile this discrepancy and perhaps reject their initial hypothesis. It is through this *process of reconciliation* where new insights are gained and changes in beliefs occur.

....

New insights are gained and changes in beliefs occur through a *process of reconciliation*. Teams and individuals reconcile the discrepancy between initial thinking and new ideas that emerge through the examination of evidence.

....

Observations About Current Theories of Action

Educators across North America are integrating theories of action into school improvement processes. In many school districts, the articulation of a theory of action has become integral to the creation of district and school improvement plans. Collaborative inquiry teams are also formulating theories of action. In cases where instructional rounds are occurring, it is not uncommon for theories to be articulated as well. The idea of creating and sharing a theory of action is spreading widely. We encounter school districts' theories of action in the school improvement work we support across the province of Ontario. In addition, we have witnessed school districts in the United States and other provinces in Canada developing theories of action related to system and school improvement.

In the introductory chapter of *The Six Secrets of Change*, entitled "Have Theory, Will Travel," Fullan (2008) pointed out that "theories that travel well are those that practically and insightfully guide the understanding of complex situations and point to actions likely to be effective under the circumstances" (p. 1). We have come to the conclusion that while the idea of creating a theory of action has *traveled well*, the theories themselves are not compelling enough to *travel well*. Many of the theories we encounter are both broad in nature and do not contain the insight needed for dealing with complex issues related to improving student learning. The following are a few examples:

- *If* we provide descriptive feedback, *then* student achievement will increase.
- *If* we use ICT in the classroom, *then* students will be more engaged.
- *If* we remove the photocopier, *then* teachers will adopt more constructivist teaching approaches.

As you can see, because of the ambiguous nature of these theories, there is no clear linkage between the *if* and the *then*. These theories do not point to actions likely to be effective.

••

We have come to the conclusion that while the idea of creating a theory of action has *traveled well*, the theories themselves are not compelling enough to *travel well*.

••

What is equally disconcerting is that the purpose for developing a theory of action is often misunderstood and/or unrealized. In discussions with administrators, when asked why they are developing a theory of action as part of their school improvement plan, we are often met with a puzzled look and the following responses: "Oh, do you mean the 'if/then' statement? Well, we create one because it's part of the school improvement template," or "I do it because my superintendent asked me to." The section that follows offers considerations for collaborative inquiry teams in developing a theory of action that will be robust enough to travel well.

Developing a Theory of Action That Will Travel Well

Fullan (2008) noted that "the question of effectiveness is not how smart you are; it is about how *grounded* and *insightful* your theorizing is" (p. 2). Fullan (2008) also noted that a good theory (one that travels well) helps to "make sense of the real world and are tested against it" (p. 1). There are two elements to developing a theory of action that will travel well: Remove the ambiguity by ensuring theories are explicitly articulated, and identify the assumptions that are implicitly incorporated in order to ensure the theory is grounded and insightful enough to survive professional scrutiny.

Theories that are too broad in nature do not serve the first purpose for creating them (removing the ambiguity from a collaborative inquiry team's vision of change). There is a need to replace the "black box" with a "glass box" in order to uncover the essential steps and critical elements that will or will not render the theory a success. There is a need to "unpack" theories that are too broad in nature so that they become more explicit.

Figure 3.2 Black Box/Glass Box

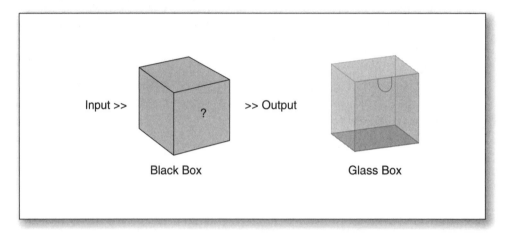

Input >>   ? >> Output

Black Box   Glass Box

Consider the following theory of action:

- *If* teachers engage in collaborative inquiry as an approach to professional learning, *then* they will identify student-learning needs and share their challenges of practice.
- *If* teachers determine their learning needs based on identified gaps in student learning, *then* professional learning will be differentiated, more precise, and applicable.
- *If* teachers share their teaching practices and resulting student learning with each other, *then* they will be able to draw upon each other's experience and expertise and develop more common understandings.
- *If* teachers reflect on their theories of action, *then* they will monitor the impact of their actions.
- *If* teachers incorporate new approaches based on research and the learning needs of their students, *then* students will benefit from more effective teaching and student achievement will increase.

While this series of statements might appear to be several theories of action, it is actually one unpacked theory. The example demonstrates a clearer path toward the desired outcome (increasing student achievement), making more explicit what each action is intended to produce.

When teams of educators come together to formulate theories of action, it would be beneficial for them to consider the specificity of their theory. Has the team mapped out the sequence of strategic actions they feel are needed to address complex issues? In other words, has the team replaced the black box (and then a miracle occurs) with a glass box in order to make their thinking and rationale transparent to all?

Sparks (2007) referred to a theory of action as "a set of underlying assumptions about how the organization will move from its current state to its desired future" (p. 38). Sparks (2007) cautioned that "these assumptions affect improvement efforts whether they are hidden from us because we have never consciously considered them or are explicit because we have thoughtfully reflected upon their efficacy and articulated them to others" (p. 38). After articulating causal statements, teams identify assumptions that are implicit in their theory. Identifying assumptions is important for many reasons. As a result, underlying beliefs and values that drive the team's actions are surfaced. Understanding different assumptions helps teams to work together more effectively. The process also helps to uncover possible things teams have not considered that need to be in place (or avoided) in order to meet with success. For example, one team who planned to use a think-aloud approach to improving students' ability to form and support opinions uncovered the important assumptions that all students are auditory learners and that the team shared a common understanding of the think-aloud strategy. Obviously, not all students are auditory learners, and while uncovering the assumption that a common understanding of thinking-aloud existed amongst team members, the group discovered that they had very different ideas about this approach. While uncovering assumptions, team members often discover that they do not share common understandings, and this realization becomes the springboard for identifying professional learning and developing shared meaning.

The following are a few assumptions embedded in the theory of action shared above:

- Student-learning needs are accurately identified.
- Teachers are willing to expose their challenges of practice.
- Professional learning will ensue (teachers will gain new knowledge and skills).
- New knowledge and skills will be put into practice.
- New practices identified will have an impact on students.

As noted by Sparks (2007), we must reflect on the efficacy of our theories. For example, an elementary school's strategy to improve numeracy in the primary grades may be the creation of a "Family Take Home Activity Bag." Contained in the bag might be a few children's books focused on mathematics-related concepts, manipulatives, and math games. Assumptions embedded in the school's theory of action include the following: that students' numeracy achievement will improve for all or most students because of parental engagement; math games contained in the activity bag are adequately effective and when used at home will improve numeracy; parents will read the books aloud and play the math games with their children; parents will know what to do with the manipulatives; and so forth. As this example illustrates, when engaging in thoughtful assumption identification, teams often discover that they are using relatively weak interventions to pursue substantial goals.

> When teams do not identify assumptions embedded in their theories, they run the risk of pursuing lofty goals through the use of comparatively weak interventions. Assumption identification enables teams to examine the efficacy of their theorizing and revise theories to ensure for more grounded and insightful theorizing, prior to taking action. In addition, it is a springboard to identifying educator learning and developing common understandings.

Revisiting and Revising Theories of Action

Once theories are developed and assumptions are identified, teams engage in professional practice to test their theories and assumptions. Fullan (2011) referred to this as "deliberative doing" (p. 5) and noted it as the core-learning method for effective leaders. This is the experimentation aspect of a theory of action. It is in testing the theory through experimentation that the team reshapes their theories based on their experiences and the experiences of their colleagues. This is what Argyris and Schön (1978) refer to as "double-loop learning." Through reflection, individuals discover incongruencies between their current theories of action and how their theories actually play out in reality. Double-loop learning occurs when theories are revised and underlying assumptions, values, and beliefs are modified. This is why Katz and Dack (2013) refer to collaborative inquiry as "an enabler of the kind of professional learning that is about permanent change in thinking or behavior" (p. 7). This reflective insight guides further action, as teams continue to test, revisit, and revise theories accordingly. Strategies for engaging team members in double-loop learning are expanded on in Chapter 4.

Reeves (2011) noted that "while focus alone is not a sufficient strategy for school improvement, focus is a prerequisite for improvement" (p. 4). The author revealed through a multivariate analysis that when "focus is combined with other variables—such as effective monitoring, professional learning, assessment and feedback—then student achievement gains are more than five times greater than when a failure to focus prevents success-ful teaching and leadership" (p. 4). We must ensure that collaborative inquiry teams focus on what matters the most—student-learning needs. Careful consideration must be made to composition of teams. Inquiries must come from a place of authenticity. Ambiguity must be removed from theories of action, and assumptions must be uncovered to ensure that the-ories are grounded and insightful.

In addition to determining and maintaining a meaningful focus, facil-itators must provoke thinking, so that team members assess the impact of their actions on student outcomes. This includes building an appreciation for an educator's capacity to use a variety of assessment data, collabora-tively analyzing student work, determining the next best move, and recon-ciling discrepancies in theories of action. These ideas are expanded on in the next chapter.

4 Provoking Thinking to Assess Impact

"Leaders must have conversations that interrogate reality, provoke learning, tackle tough challenges and enrich relationships" (Scott, 2004, p. xix).

Figure 4.1   Provoking Thinking to Assess Impact

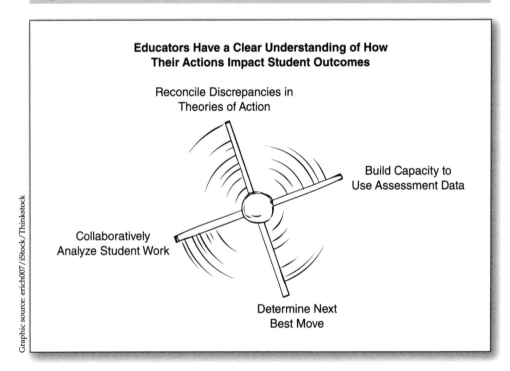

E ducators hold different beliefs about the scope of their influence and their ability to impact student outcomes. These efficacy beliefs can be increased as a result of participating in collaborative inquiry (Bruce & Flynn, 2013; Cooper-Twamley, 2009; Galligan, 2011; Henson, 2001; Voelkel Jr., 2011). Over time, team members come to see the positive impacts they have on students and attribute it, in part, to their collective action. Hattie (personal communication, November 19, 2015) ranked collective teacher efficacy as the number one factor influencing student achievement and noted that it is a powerful precursor to student success.

> "Schools that engage in collaborative inquiry develop a sense of collective efficacy that helps educators reconnect with their original point of passion: ensuring student success" (Langer & Colton, 2005, p. 26).

The collaborative inquiry cycle necessitates ongoing conversation and reflection among participants focused on assessing the impact of their actions on student learning. Compelling educators to measure, consider, and share with colleagues how their teaching practice *is* or *is not* impacting students is one of the most difficult stages to support in the cycle of inquiry. It is a risky *independent* endeavor, let alone when done publicly. However, research demonstrates it is a vital step in developing a professional learning culture and transforming learning, leading, and teaching (Kazemi & Franke, 2004; Nelson, 2008).

Ways to provoke the thinking necessary for educators to critically analyze the impact their actions have on student learning will be explored in this chapter. These include building the team's appreciation for and their capacity to use a variety of assessment data. As new approaches are implemented in classrooms, it is beneficial for teams to frequently and collaboratively examine student-learning evidence as it helps to determine next steps for both students who are struggling and for those who are excelling. In order to determine whether or not the team had an impact, teams need to know what outcomes resulted and how and why the existing outcomes were achieved. In addition, individuals and teams will need to reconcile discrepancies between espoused theories and theories-in-use. Strategies and tools for doing so are explored in this chapter.

BUILDING APPRECIATION FOR AND CAPACITY TO USE A VARIETY OF ASSESSMENT DATA

When participants begin this process, one of the problematic areas is in identifying and collecting evidence that is triangulated, valid, and reliable. Although teams set out with the best intentions, when they come together to analyze evidence, they often find that they are drowning in data and are unsure what it all means. When facilitators ensure that teams focus on evidence that will help answer their inquiry question and examine it frequently and collaboratively, it helps to strengthen this stage in the cycle.

Types of Data That Can Be Used for School Improvement

When determining evidence that will assist in answering inquiry questions, teams benefit from considering four types of data that can be used for school improvement (Bernhardt, 2000). These include student-learning data, demographic data, school-process data, and perceptual data. In the section that follows, the types of data are described followed by a list of questions (see also Resource A) that facilitators might use to help the team determine how each type of data may or may not be useful in their inquiries. While it is not an exhaustive list, the questions are designed to help ensure that the evidence collected is both valid and reliable.

> Validity: Ask the question: Are we measuring what we think we are measuring?
>
> Reliability: Ask the question: If we were to repeat this, would we get the same results?

Student-Learning Data

Student-learning data includes the day-to-day assessments and evaluations teachers make about student learning. Sources include student work products, observations, and conversations. Standardized tests also provide a rich source of student-learning data. Bernhardt (2000) noted that student-learning data tell schools which students are succeeding academically and which are not. This is an important source of evidence for collaborative inquiry teams, as it helps them to consider current results—how are our students doing right now? This information is critical in guiding next steps, including determining the next best move and the professional learning needs of educators. When examined frequently, teams are able to adjust instruction accordingly and identify which students are succeeding and which students require additional supports and scaffolding.

Questions to Consider: Student-Learning Data

Facilitators should encourage participants to consider collecting student-learning data obtained through a variety of means, including day-to-day observations, conversations, and student work products. Below is a list of questions that, depending on the team's needs, facilitators could pose:

- Do team members share a common understanding of the student-learning need that has been identified?
- What would the student-learning evidence look like if students were performing at the highest level? Lowest level? Somewhere in between?
- Does the evidence measure student learning or is it measuring something else?
- What are different ways to collect evidence that could reflect potential changes in student learning over time?
- How and when will team members collect student-learning data?
- Is evidence formative or summative in nature? Does this matter? If so, why?

Demographic Data

Demographic data include information related to the school context and how it might change over time. Enrollment, attendance, first language spoken at home, number of students with individual education plans, percentage of students in applied or academic pathways, percentage of students receiving free and/or reduced lunch, and teacher's qualifications are some examples of demographic data. These data provide the overarching context for everything that the school does with respect to school improvement (Bernhardt, 2000). Collaborative inquiry teams could use demographic data to help inform whether they are achieving greater success for *all* students. They may also use it to determine the allocation of resources and to pinpoint where to provide additional supports.

Questions to Consider: Demographic Data

Demographic data will help teams compare and analyze subgroups to see how the outcomes vary between groups;

- Which groups of students do teams need to carefully consider, given the identified student-learning need?
- Does the collaborative inquiry team know which groups of students are high performing? Low performing? At-risk? If not, how can the team find out?

School Process Data

Bernhardt (2000) described school processes data as the curriculum, instruction and assessment strategies, programs and interventions, and any other classroom approaches that teachers use to help students learn. In order to strengthen the collaborative inquiry process, it is important to document and examine school process data. Gathering information about school processes is one way teams could monitor the degree of implementation of practices. It is also necessary to collect in order for team members to make sense of their actions and assess the effects of their work.

Questions to Consider: School Process Data

This is the measure that seems to be the hardest for collaborative inquiry teams to describe and document. As noted by Bernhardt (2000), most often teams say they do what they do intuitively:

- What school processes (most likely classroom practices) are collaborative inquiry teams identifying as a means to address gaps in student learning?
- How does this new practice differ from teacher's regular practice? (Is it really a change?)
- Is there a research base to support the new practice?
- Do team members share a common understanding of new instructional approaches?
- What additional knowledge and skills do educators need in order to implement new approaches?
- How will you know the new practice was implemented?
- How will you know to what level it was implemented?
- What supports do teachers need to "stay the course" (given it is the "right" course)?

Perceptual Data

Perceptual data tell us about how satisfied students, parents, educators, and the larger community are with the work of the school (Bernhardt, 2000). Perceptual data can help collaborative inquiry teams in understanding how their efforts are meeting the learning needs of students, by examining feelings and opinions in regard to changes in practice. Perceptual data can be gathered in a variety of ways, including questionnaires and interviews from a variety of sources, including students, parents, and educators.

Questions to Consider: Perceptual Data

Often, collaborative inquiry teams collect perceptual data that does not pertain to their question. Although perceptual data can be very valuable, teams must consider its relevance in relation to their inquiry question:

- Does the team's inquiry require the collection of perceptions? If so, whose?
- How will the collection of perceptual data help the team answer its question?
- If collected, what is this information going to tell us? How will it help advance the work of the team?

Factors That Influence Data Collection

A number of factors influence data collection. These include the inquiry question itself, teacher's beliefs about the nature and quality of evidence, and available time and resources. Leaders and facilitators should increase their familiarity of these factors, so they can raise the team's collectiveness awareness when these issues with data surface throughout the inquiry.

The Inquiry Question

While some elements of research are incorporated into collaborative inquiry, it is first and foremost a design for professional learning. If this book were about conducting research in schools, it would contain information about different research designs, directions on how to form a hypothesis, and information about controlling for variables. There would be a heavy focus on probable cause and effect and assessing difference and magnitude. Since we envision collaborative inquiry as a high quality professional learning design rather than a research methodology, the research aspect is not experimental in nature, rather it is more exploratory—focused on the descriptive (What is happening?), the interpretive (What does it mean?), and process oriented (What is going on over time?).

Quality questions tend to be more open ended, beginning with words like *how* and *what* rather than *did* or *can*. Since the inquiry question will drive the data collection, the open-ended nature of the question will invite teams to consider a variety of evidence, including data obtained through observations, conversations, and student work products. Questions that begin with *did* or *can* require simple yes or no answers and often value pretest and posttest data. Ensuring questions are phrased in an exploratory way will help the team develop a triangulated data collection plan.

Teacher's Beliefs

The types of evidence teachers' value can influence the data they gather during an inquiry cycle. If teachers highly value data garnered through pencil and paper tests, then they might focus their data collection efforts on testing results. They might also identify standardized tests as a measure of impact. While this is a valuable data source, a caution is that standardized tests are often not administered frequently enough to enable teams to use the data in a responsive and timely way. This does not mean they should be discounted. Teams should consider, however, the frequency of administration when identifying what evidence they are going to collect. Is the data a trailing indicator, or are team members able to use the information in order to address current student-learning needs?

If team members value qualitative evidence, they are likely more open to considering a variety of artifacts that can serve as documentation of student learning (e.g., portfolios and performances, etc.). Examining qualitative evidence can be time consuming. Teams might select detailed information from a small number of students or individual learners over time. Strategies for examining student evidence are shared later in this chapter.

Time and Resources

Other factors that influence a collaborative inquiry team's data collection are time and resources. Teams need to consider how and when information is going to be collected and by whom. It is important for team members to see how collecting evidence fits into their daily routines. If it becomes too onerous, team members might become frustrated and give up at this stage in the cycle.

When collaborative inquiry participants are involved in identifying what evidence to collect, they are more likely to pay attention to the data, as they helped determine its importance. Building an appreciation for and capacity to use a variety of assessment data begins with making participants aware of different types of data and the factors that influence data collection.

Building a Sustainable Improvement Culture

Simon Feasey, head teacher at Bader Primary School located in Thornaby-on-Tees, England, recently described how collaborative inquiry is helping to shift performance management from the personal to a more collegiate responsibility (personal communication, November 8, 2015). In order to build a sustainable improvement culture where quality improvement was not seen as a project but an ongoing function, Feasey engaged teacher teams at Bader Primary School in ongoing cycles of collaborative inquiry. Feasey envisioned the engagement of key participants as problem definers and problem solvers as a starting point for adopting a collaborative approach to school improvement. Feasey noted that one of the strengths in the collaborative inquiry framework is that the impact measurement is something that inquiry teams fathom and design for themselves, based on identified desirable outcomes. Quoting Bryk, Gomez, Grunow, and LeMahieu (2015), Feasey noted that collaborative inquiry allows teams to "get better at getting better" and that participants "see the system that produces the current outcomes." Feasey highlighted the importance in doing so, noting that it is hard to improve a system when not fully understanding how it currently operates to produce its results.

TEACHER LEARNING THROUGH THE COLLABORATIVE ANALYSIS OF STUDENT WORK

As new practices are being tried and tested, teams use student artifacts to track progress and develop deeper understandings of how to support student learning. Examining student work helps to strengthen connections between the learning task, content, instruction, and student outcomes. Collaborative analysis helps teachers develop better understandings of how students learn, as it "invites multiple interpretations of the same event" (Langer & Colton, 2005). It helps individuals understand their own work, by drawing on the team's social capital (the collaborative power of the group). Kazemi and Franke (2004) conducted a study that focused on what teachers learn through the collective examination of student work and noted that "centering the activity on teachers' own student work allowed for conversations that deepened as well as challenged teachers' notions

> Given, Kuh, LeeKeenan, Mardell, Redditt, and Twombly (2010) noted that "meeting regularly to consider children's work and its implications for classroom practice was a fundamental step in forming communities of learners and reflecting upon teacher practice" (p. 40).

about their work as teachers" (p. 230). Furthermore, Nelson (2008) noted that a key component in a collaborative inquiry teams' progress toward reculturing the nature of their professional activities was when they collectively analyzed student work.

While examining student work holds huge promises in transforming learning, leading, and teaching, collaboratively analyzing student evidence is a big hurdle for some teams. Our observations during this stage in the cycle are that participants are sometimes reluctant to share student artifacts with each other and often speak in generalizations about student-learning outcomes. Especially when teams are new to the process, having had little experience engaging in collaborative inquiry, it is not uncommon to hear comments from participants such as, "I think it made a difference" and "It definitely worked; the students were much more engaged" and "Yes, I saw a difference. Students did much better this time." Often these statements are void of any evidence to substantiate such claims. While it is more frequently common for teachers to evaluate their lessons on students' learning in isolation, collaboratively analyzing student-learning data throughout the inquiry cycle is an important step in moving teams forward. It is a necessary step in collectively determining both the impact of changed practice and the next best move to employ. Roblin and Margalef (2013) found that "only when teachers—with time— were able to witness the impact of the new strategies on their own students' learning as well as on the results obtained by their colleagues, they started to 'let go,' embrace the uncertainty derived from the new activities, and take the challenge of exploring its potential" (p. 27).

"But before I join the chorus of 'this too shall pass' and vow to wait out the next administrative requirement, I must turn the lens inward and ask the question every true professional must ask: 'Is my present practice as effective as I think it is?' As teachers, we must be willing to confront this question every day of our professional lives if teacher leadership is to become a reality rather than a slogan" (Reeves, 2008, p. 50).

When facilitating teams through this stage in the process, the facilitator's aim is to shift conversations from generalized talk about student's progress and polite sharing of teaching strategies to more in-depth conversations about the connections between the two (Nelson, Deuel, Slavit, & Kennedy, 2010). As mentioned earlier, it is risky for teachers to collectively analyze student work. Participants are usually concerned that the process will surface questions related to professional expertise as the learning and progress of students served by individual teachers is at the forefront. In addition, there is the potential that uncertainties regarding content knowledge, pedagogy, and curriculum might be uncovered. Relationships characterized by trust are very important. Developing trust is addressed in greater detail in Chapter 5. Facilitators can also support teams by introducing the process using anonymous student work, help to manage the work by focusing the team on one or a few students of interest, and build safety by utilizing protocols and question sets. These facilitative strategies will help maintain trust and establish a nonthreatening environment.

Strategies for Examining Student Work

Begin by Using Anonymous Student Work

When introducing teams to the process, facilitators might begin with anonymous student work samples collected from within the group or gathered from other sources. Nelson (2008) found that when teachers began their examination of student work using anonymous samples, their confidence was built and it helped make the transition to collectively analyzing their own students' work less risky.

Focus on One or a Few Students of Interest

Langer and Colton (2005) suggested that "collaborative inquiry is most powerful when teachers look at an individual learner's progress over time" (p. 22). Their approach involves diagnosing student-learning needs and then selecting a focus student who represents a common challenge found through the examination of student-learning data. Next, as collaborative inquiry team members experiment with various instructional practices, they continue to analyze a different focus **on** student's work samples each week to "learn why that student was (or was not) making progress in the identified area" (p. 23). The authors suggested that "because the focus students represent a cluster of students who exhibit similar learning challenges, teachers can use what they learn from studying one student with the larger group" (p. 23). Langer and Colton (2005) also noted an additional advantage in studying one student over a period of time is that "teachers often discover gaps in their own knowledge based when their teaching strategies fail" (p. 24), leading to an identification of their own professional learning needs. Again, it is at this point that teachers make recursive loops through the inquiry cycle. The collaborative analysis of student work is pivotal in driving the learning forward.

Introduce Protocols for Analyzing Student Work

Facilitators can introduce protocols in order to ensure team members feel safe in publicly sharing student results. Protocols structure conversations in a way that helps teams maintain objectivity and focus.

"The structures in protocols are not usually novel; their value comes from making the rules of interaction explicit—they establish that the group is accountable to each other, and they provide the means for facilitators and participants to hold a group to their agreements. Protocols help people practice the skills they espouse but that they don't always know how to enact" (City et al., 2009, p. 76).

Sample Questions provided by Nelson et al. (2010) include the following:

- What do you see or hear that suggests students understand/almost understand/do not understand?
- How do students' responses relate to the lesson taught?
- What patterns in students' work suggest I/we should continue teaching this way, make some modifications, or try to use a different approach?

Facilitators could use these questions as examples. As a next step, the team develops its own questions and refers to them as needed.

Many protocols offer advice on the criteria for selecting specific work to analyze. They also provide advice to facilitators and suggest time lines to adhere to. A number of books are devoted to this topic. In addition, a number of protocols for examining student work (along with anonymous samples of student work) can be found online.

Develop Question Sets

As mentioned earlier, it is our experience that individuals talk in generalities when first sharing evidence of impact on student learning. Facilitators might shy away from asking critical questions about how approaches are impacting students and what evidence team members have to support claims. Nelson et al. (2010) offered a safe way to surface these questions through group-generated question sets. Group-generated sets of questions can be used as a safe and agreed upon way to delve deeper into connections between learning and teaching. Questions are generated in advance by the team. Their purpose is to ensure the team draws connections between the student learning and teaching. Once they are developed by the team, they are posted to act as a reminder and a place to turn if the conversation becomes unfocused, too subjective, or too general.

When collaborative inquiry teams engage in the collaborative analysis of student work, it results in increased teaching effectiveness and student success. Teams use artifacts of student work to better understand students' thinking, uncover misconceptions, and identify strengths and areas for improvement. Based on this information, teams determine how to respond and what adjustments to make to their practice. Whether this happens or not depends on the actual use of student-learning artifacts.

Support is critical to help develop the trust needed to share student work and assist teams in making sense of student work in relation to their instructional practice and student learning.

DETERMINING NEXT BEST MOVE

Student-learning data is analyzed in order to determine the team's next best move. At this point, teams are likely to make recursive loops through the inquiry cycle. Participants continue to deepen their professional knowledge and refine their skills as they engage learners in new experiences and continue to collectively assess the impact of those changes (Figure 1.2). A team member once asked us, "How do you know when it's time to move on? When is the inquiry over?" In considering a proper response to that question, the Results Path (Figure 4.2) was developed. This tool enables team members to consider their actions and resulting student outcomes and provides prompts to assist the team in determining their next steps.

The Results Path

The Results Path is a tool that facilitators can use to help teams reflect on their results to date and trace their current reality down one of four possible pathways. Teams first determine whether the results from the collaborative inquiry showed an improvement in student outcomes or no improvement in student outcomes. Next, if there was an improvement in student outcomes as a result of the inquiry, participants select one of two pathways. If the team has no understanding of how or why the results were achieved, they would follow the Path 1. If the team has a clear understanding of how or why the results were achieved, they would follow the Path 2.

"Teachers with professional capital are not driven by data or overly dependent on measurable evidence—but they do inquire into, identify, and adapt the best ways for moving forward, making intelligent, critical, and reflective use of measurable evidence and considered experience alike. And they are committed to knowing and showing what impact they have on their students, and to fulfilling their responsibility for making this transparent to the public they serve" (Hargreaves & Fullan, 2012, p. 49).

"Not critical reflection, but *critical reflection in light of evidence* about their teaching" (Hattie, 2012, p.19).

The collaborative inquiry process does not cease, rather it becomes an ongoing effort to build greater collective capacity in regard to improving student outcomes. Once teams move beyond a focus on how to "do" inquiry, they engage in self-sustaining cycles of inquiry.

Figure 4.2   Results Path

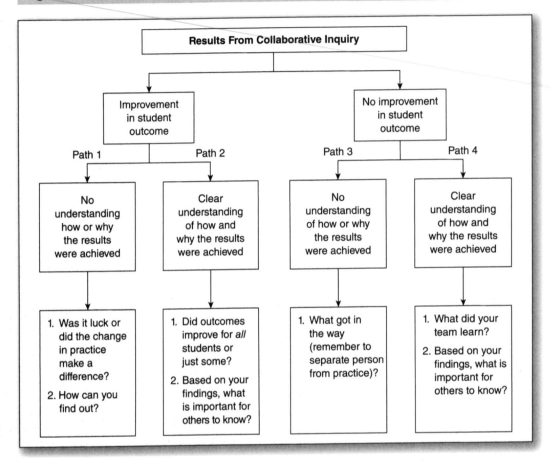

Alternatively, if there was no improvement in student outcomes, participants select either Path 3 or Path 4. Teams who have no understanding as to how or why no changes in student learning resulted, follow Path 3. Teams who have a clear understanding as to how or why the results were achieved (that is no improvement in student outcomes) follow Path 4.

Teams who can trace their inquiries along Path 1 (improvement in student outcomes with no understanding as to how or why) are asked to consider the following questions: Was it luck or did the change in practice make a difference? How can teams find out?

Teams along Path 2 (improvement in student learning with a clear understanding as to how or why) are asked to consider the following questions: Did outcomes improve for all students or just some? Based on your findings, what is important for others to know?

Teams tracing their inquiries along Path 3 (no improvement in student learning with no understanding as to how or why) are asked to consider the following questions: What got in the way? (Remember to separate person from practice.)

Finally, teams following Path 4 (no improvement in student learning with a clear understanding as to how or why) are asked to consider the following questions: What did your team learn? Based on your findings, what is important for others to know?

There are times when a team might realize they are heading down a different path altogether—sometimes they do not know whether

> Note: The Results Path was conceived based on Reeves' (2010) Leadership and Learning Matrix. Those familiar with Reeves' Leadership and Learning Matrix will see the similarities between it and the Results Path.

their actions resulted in an increase in student outcomes or not. If teams come to this realization, facilitators can reengage teams by cycling back to consider evidence of implementation (school process data) and student artifacts (student-learning data). When teams reflect on their results in relation to the different paths, it helps them to refocus and determine next steps. Teams cycle through the inquiry process by redefining the problem and their focus in light of new understandings and evidence. Once teachers begin to attribute increases in student outcomes to their own efforts, the collaborative inquiry process is recognized as pivotal to school improvement and worth the investment.

Hattie (2012) pointed out that "evidence of impact or not may mean that teachers need to modify or dramatically change their theories of action" (p. 4). In addition to using the Results Path to assess impact, facilitators engage teams in reflective practice and change the nature of conversations in order to support a reconstruction of theories of action. These ideas are expanded on in the section that follows.

RECONCILING DISCREPANCIES: THEORIES OF ACTION

As noted earlier, mental maps are the consciously or unconsciously held beliefs that guide our actions (Argyris and Schön, 1978). Contrasting theories of action are espoused theories and theories-in-use. Espoused theories are those in which we claim to follow how we think we behave in certain circumstances. Theories-in-use can be inferred from our actions—in other words, how we actually behave in certain circumstances. Argyris and Schön (1978) advocated for critical examination of theories of action (espoused theories versus theories-in-use) when trying to solve dilemmas or dealing with conflicts related to practice—in other words, when trying to solve adaptive challenges. Reflecting on the practice of teaching and/or the practice of leading takes place in the interest of collectively learning about how to bring theories-in-use in line with espoused theories.

∙∙

Reflecting on the practice of teaching and/or the practice of leading takes place in the interest of collectively learning about how to bring theories-in-use in line with espoused theories.

∙∙

Numerous studies that examine the extent to which educators' beliefs are manifested in their practice reveal discrepancies between espoused theories and theories-in-use. For example, Lee (2009) examined the extent to which teachers' written feedback practices corresponded with their beliefs and found ten mismatches (e.g., teachers use error codes, although they think students have a limited ability to decipher codes). Irvin (1999) found incongruence between how a teacher perceived her role (facilitator) and her actions (show and direct) in teaching composition in a high school English classroom. In examining the research on learner autonomy, Watkins (n.d.) stated "it would be wrong to suggest that reasons for low pupil autonomy are that teachers do not value it" (p. 28) and noted that "evidence shows that promoting learners' autonomy is where the gap is biggest between current classroom practice and teachers' values" (p. 29).

In our collaborative inquiry work with educators, we have witnessed the changes in thinking and behavior that result when the incongruence between theories of action are uncovered. One of us worked recently with a teacher who placed high value on collaboration and believed that by providing opportunities for students to talk to each other about their learning, their understanding would be enhanced. Therefore, students were seated in groups or pairs in his classroom. In examining his actual practice, he realized that students spent more than 80% of their time doing individual activities. In another example, a superintendent espoused that advancing opportunities for teacher leadership was one of her top priorities. In examining her leadership practice, she realized that some of her actions actually impeded opportunities for teachers to take on leadership responsibilities. Coming to the realization that there was a gap between their beliefs and practices allowed both these educators to put steps in place to reduce the gap.

Hattie (2012) cautioned that "theories have purposes as tools for synthesizing notions, but too often teachers believe that theories dictate action, even when the evidence of impact does not support their particular theories (and then maintaining their theories almost becomes a religion)" (p. 4). A critical aspect in reconciling discrepancies in theories is in bringing to light the incongruence. In Chapter 3, we discussed the idea of developing a theory of action that will travel well. In this chapter we delve further in exploring and reflecting on the efficacy of our theories. Suggestions for examining professional practice via theories of action are shared in the section that follows. In order to reconcile discrepancies between theories-in-use and theories espoused, we need to extend thinking about practice through reflection and change the nature of everyday conversations.

Extending Thinking About Practice Through Reflection

Schön (1983) emphasized the importance of reflection as a key element in professional growth. Reflection leads to increased self-awareness, a broader understanding of adaptive challenges, and the generation of new knowledge about professional practice. Since it is an important element to improving practice, collaborative inquiry teams benefit when reflection is intentionally elicited and time is provided for team members to reflect together. When reflection takes place in a public forum, team members gain a greater understanding of others as well as a greater understanding of themselves.

Reflection involves stepping back and identifying aspects of professional practice that are worthy of analysis. Teams use theories of action, student-learning data, and school process data as a starting point. Team members determine what is different about their practice and its impact, and in light of the evidence, they reexamine assumptions and may revise their initial theories. Facilitators need to ensure that team members not only make sense of what has been learned from the experience but that they also determine if the experience has created a permanent change in the individuals and/or the team.

· ·

Facilitators need to ensure that team members not only make sense of what has been learned from experience but that they also determine if the experience has created a permanent change in the individuals and/or the team.

· ·

We have found the Reflecting on Practice template (Resource B) helpful in guiding reflective conversations. An individual completes the column on the left, answering each of the five questions. Then, as the individual shares his or her answer to each question, the collaborative inquiry team completes the column on the right.

Figure 4.3 Resource B—Reflecting on Practice

Individual	Collective
What was different from my regular practice?	What elements were the same as what we do in our practice?
What went well?	Why did it go well?
What did not go well?	Why did it not go well?
What have I learned?	What lessons can we take away from this that will inform our practice?
What (if anything) will I permanently change in my practice?	What (if anything) will we permanently change in our practice?

Reflecting on Theories of Action (Resource C) is another template that can be used to engage teams in reflective practice. Teams complete the chart together, contemplating each question row by row.

Both templates were designed to help facilitators uncover individual experiences and bring them out into the open. In order to maximize collective learning through reflection, participants need to contextually locate themselves within their individual experiences then collaboratively explore available theory, knowledge, and collective expertise to understand individual experiences in different ways. The templates also help in developing professional capital, as they honor the talent of individuals (human capital), take advantage of the collaborative power of the group (social capital), and draw on collective expertise for making sound judgments (decisional capital) (Hargreaves & Fullan, 2012, p. 5). The questions help teams consider their theories and assumptions.

Senge, Scharmer, Jaworski, and Flowers (2004) noted that "breakthroughs come when people learn how to take the time to stop and examine their assumptions" (p. 33). Finally, Elmore (2008) noted that "a central part of the practice of improvement should be to make the connection between teaching practice and student learning more direct and clear" (p. 129). The templates are designed to make this connection more explicit.

Garmston (2012) noted that "all groups possess collective mental models" (p. 94) and shared facilitation strategies and protocols to illuminate mental models. One strategy Garmston (2012) referred to is a Causal-Loop Diagram (p. 102). When completed, it displays multiple cause-and-effect loops. On sticky notes, individuals write what they feel the group should

Figure 4.4 Resource C—Reflecting on Theories of Action

What is the ideal?	What is real?
What was expected?	What occurred?
What actions were taken?	What were the reasons for the action?
What are alternative strategies?	What is the next best move?
What new assumptions are arising?	What do we need to learn more about?

improve, and on separate sticky notes, individuals list possible factors that are holding the team back. Once posted, the team works collaboratively to cluster the notes and identify cause-and-effect loops. Garmston (2012) noted that "patterns that emerge" help collaborative inquiry teams "identify mental models driving their work" (p. 103). This allows team members to examine them and modify them accordingly.

James and Pedder (2006) designed and utilized a dual-scale questionnaire in order to elicit teachers' perceptions of current practices and the value they place on those practices. Teachers were asked to make two kinds of responses. The first referenced whether particular practices were never true, rarely true, often true, or mostly true in their school and/or classroom (uncovering theories-in-use). The second scale focused on values. Teachers were asked to indicate "how important they felt the given practice was in creating opportunities for students to learn" (114). Response categories for the second scale ranged from "not at all important" to "crucial" (theories espoused). The researchers found the dual-scale questionnaire a useful strategy for identifying the gap between what teachers practiced and what they valued.

Resource D (on the following page) includes statements that are reflective of assessment *for* learning practices (center column) and demonstrates the two Likert-type scales (Scale X and Scale Y). Although assessment *for* learning is included as an example, the questionnaire could easily be redesigned to include statements reflective of other educational practices.

Regardless of the structure, whether utilizing a template, a protocol, or a questionnaire, it is the conversation that really matters. Specific tools are helpful only to the degree in which they are purposefully selected and adhered to. Facilitators make use of templates and protocols to aid in focusing discussion, making sense of experiences, and reconstructing beliefs. When appropriately selected and utilized true to their design, templates and protocols can be very useful tools in fulfilling a specific purpose. However, they cannot be relied on to transform *every* conversation. Ultimately, it is individuals who must take on the responsibility for doing so.

Figure 4.5   Resource D—Identifying the Gap: Practice and Values

Scale X This school now. My classroom now. (About Your Practice)				Assessment for Learning	Scale Y How important are your assessment practices for creating opportunities for students to learn? (About Your Values)				
Never True	Rarely True	Often True	Mostly True		Not important at all	Of limited importance	Important	Crucial	Bad Practice
Never True	Rarely True	Often True	Mostly True	1. Explicitly sharing learning intentions and success criteria so that they could be used as a point of reference for feedback.	Not important at all	Of limited importance	Important	Crucial	Bad Practice
Never True	Rarely True	Often True	Mostly True	2. Encouraging students to make judgments about the quality of work, based on success criteria, during its actual production.	Not important at all	Of limited importance	Important	Crucial	Bad Practice
Never True	Rarely True	Often True	Mostly True	3. Enabling students to compare their actual level of achievement with an expected standard.	Not important at all	Of limited importance	Important	Crucial	Bad Practice

Changing the Conversation

Provoking thinking to assess impact involves changing conversations that occur in schools everyday. If we are to realize a transformation in learning, leading, and teaching, the following shifts need to occur in everyday conversations:

> Bushe and Marshak (2015) noted that "change is promoted to the extent that everyday conversations are altered" (p. 17).

We need a shift from

- What has been taught to what has been learned
- Attributing results to factors outside one's control to those within it
- Fixed mindset language to growth mindset language
- Low expectations to high expectations
- Opposition to change to advocating for change
- Valuing isolation to valuing collaboration
- Certainty to inquiry

Being mindful of our own talk and modeling, what is outlined above is only a starting point. Drawing attention to the language used by others, especially when a shift is required, is necessary as well—but not easy to do. The following excerpt from Scott (2004) is how we describe the role of a skillful facilitator in regard to changing day-to-day conversations:

> My role is not to say what is easy to say or what we all can say, but to say what we have been unable to say. I try to pay attention to things that may pass unobserved by others and bring them out into the open. The most valuable thing any of us can do is find a way to say the things that can't be said. (p. 174)

When saying what is difficult to say, successful outcomes depend on how the conversation is approached. If individuals feel they are being judged, feelings of insecurity will likely result. If individuals feel they are being condescended, anger and resentment might ensue. Trust can easily break down. Garmston (2012) promoted paraphrasing and questioning as a means of finding a way to say what is difficult to say. Garmston (2012) stated that "assuming that others' intentions are positive encourages honest conversations about important matters" (p. 88) and suggested that paraphrases framed within positive presuppositions "reduce the possibility that the listener will perceive threats or challenges" (p. 88). Garmston (2012) also noted "a good question is probably the second most important language strategy a facilitator can use" (p. 164).

Garmston (2012) pointed out that when we paraphrase, we are operating within the mental maps of others. When we question, we operate from our own mental maps.

"It takes courage to start a conversation. But if we don't start talking to one another, nothing will change. Conversation is the way we discover how to transform our world, together" (Wheatley, 2002, p. 31).

Scott (2004) also shared the following insight: "It is our beliefs about what we can say, as well as how and to whom we can say it, that are in the way and that if we change our beliefs, productive conversations can easily occur" (p. 21). We encourage you to examine your beliefs about the everyday conversations that occur in your place of learning. What are your beliefs about what you can say as well as how and to whom you can say it? In addition to modeling language that is focused on assessing the impact of your actions on student outcomes, practice paraphrasing and questioning others in order to help them consider causes and effects of student learning.

As we become aware of our theories-in-use, we become more aware of contradictions between what we do and what we hope to do. By subjecting our own actions to critical assessment via reflection and changing the nature of conversations, we can collectively learn from experiences and make transformative changes in regard to learning, leading, and teaching.

We explored a number of ways to provoke the thinking necessary for educators to critically analyze the impact their actions have on student learning in this chapter. These included building the team's appreciation for and their capacity to use a variety of assessment data, strategies for collaboratively examining student learning, considerations for determining next steps, and ways to reconcile discrepancies in theories of action. In the final chapter, we consider how to shape the development of a professional learning culture.

5 Shaping the Development of a Professional Learning Culture

"Effective organizations, including schools, should make building culture part of a planned strategic effort" (Fisher, Frey, & Pumpian, 2012, p. 5).

Figure 5.1   Shaping the Development of a Professional Learning Culture

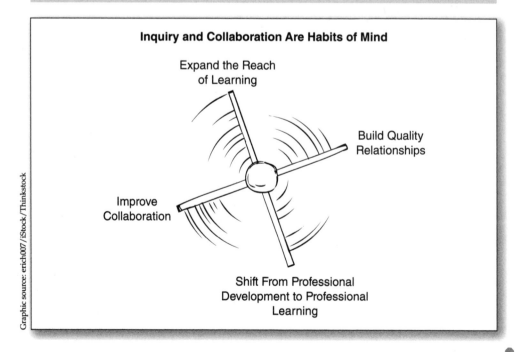

Inquiry and Collaboration Are Habits of Mind

Expand the Reach
of Learning

Build Quality
Relationships

Improve
Collaboration

Shift From Professional
Development to Professional
Learning

Graphic source: erich007/iStock/Thinkstock

Culture can be described as the deep-seated and commonly shared assumptions and values that guide decisions, communications, and relationships in schools and school districts. Culture is something individuals in organizations intuitively understand and accept. However, a rare few work toward articulating and analyzing it for the purpose of advocating for a more desirable place of work. The notion that culture can be a barrier to school improvement is not a novel idea. In fact, it is often the great enigma that holds back school improvement efforts. Therefore, it is beneficial for change agents to strategically plan to develop cultures in which educators value and advocate for high quality professional learning.

Strategically developing a culture where inquiry and collaboration are a habit of mind and teachers recognize themselves as leaders requires deliberate attention. Beginning with building an awareness of the differences between cultures of professional development and cultures for professional learning, facilitators help to set the context for deep thinking and collaborative learning. Since much of this work rests on the quality of professional relationships, understanding the complexity of helping adults, building relationships that are characterized by true partnership, and establishing and maintaining trust is important. Educators need to see collaboration as a powerful mechanism for exploring beliefs, scrutinizing practice, and getting better, and therefore, teams benefit from considering how to improve collaboration. Finally, the reach of learning must be expanded. These ideas are explored further throughout this chapter.

SHIFTING FROM PROFESSIONAL DEVELOPMENT TO PROFESSIONAL LEARNING

Commonly shared assumptions and values about the nature, content, and source for educator development have guided decisions in school districts for years. Many existing professional development cultures are rooted, arguably unintentionally, on the assumption that the responsibility of improving teaching practice rests with those who hold teachers accountable for student learning and not necessarily teachers themselves. What teachers learn about continually changes, but the real need is in changing how teachers learn. Whether it is in the content or process of teacher learning, teachers express frustration that their voices and perspectives are largely ignored (BCG Consulting, 2014). In studying teacher perceptions of professional development, Knight (n.d.) found that teachers had (a) a history of interpersonal conflict with other teachers; (b) a historical belief that professional development is impractical; (c) a feeling of being overwhelmed by the tasks they need to complete as teachers; (d) resentment about the top-down decision-making in the district; and (e) anxiety about changes taking place in their schools. Not only are teachers unsatisfied, but professional development does not guarantee changes in classroom instruction. Katz and Dack (2013) argued that "the impact of professional development on teacher practice is by no means a given" (p. 25).

> What teachers learn about continually changes, but the real need is in changing how teachers learn.

In order to empower teachers to advocate for opportunities to engage in professional learning that is powerful, there is a need to augment a shift from a professional development culture to a professional learning culture. When districts rely heavily on models of professional development (one-shot workshops where topics are determined and prioritized by central office staff), educators' needs are often not met and transfer to practice rarely occurs. More powerful professional learning designs, however, position teachers as the most authoritative voice when determining the focus, direction, and processes. Convincing teachers that they truly have this level of autonomy in collaborative inquiry might be challenging perhaps, because their experiences in professional development cultures have suggested otherwise.

The hallmarks of professional learning cultures are reflected in Learning Forward's Standards for Professional Learning. Learning Forward identified standards that can be used to guide the design, implementation, and evaluation of professional learning. "Through exploration of individual and collective experiences, learners actively construct, analyze, evaluate, and synthesize knowledge and practices" (Learning Forward, n.d.). Promoting active engagement through collaborative inquiry requires thoughtful facilitation that helps educators (a) unpack the differences between professional development and professional learning; (b) understand the relationship between change and learning; and (c) make a long-term commitment.

Unpack the Differences: Professional Development and Professional Learning

It is the facilitator's role to help teams see the value in the collaborative inquiry process as a dynamic way to engage in professional learning, especially in initial cycle iterations.

> "A school's culture should not be underground and assumed. It should be uncovered, openly and purposely discussed, assessed, and developed" (Fisher et al., 2012, p. 6).

Collaborative inquiry realizes teachers as partners in the mission to improve the learning and experiences of students. Traditionally, professional development has negated teachers' voices.

In helping the team envision a renewed culture for professional learning, facilitators will need to invest time to help teams unpack the differences between professional development and professional learning. Comparing and contrasting the two will help shape a clear purpose and identify an urgent need for more impactful professional learning practices. When teachers

Table 5.1 Differences Between Professional Development and Professional Learning

Professional Development	Professional Learning
Seeks to change teaching	Seeks to change learning
Hopes and strives for change	Ensures and plans for change
Changed behavior signals learning	Changed thinking signals learning
Delivered once or twice by an outside expert	Ongoing
Topics determined and prioritized by others	Topics determined by educators engaging in the learning and based on student-learning needs
Values • Product and performance • Breadth and reach *to many* individuals • Leadership from school and district leaders	**Values** • Processes • Depth of understanding *within* individuals • Leadership from and within teachers
Positions knowledge • Something to be disseminated • Generated only through academic pursuits (e.g., research)	**Positions knowledge** • Something to be applied and refined • Generated within and between educators
Assumes • Similar environments across all classrooms • Singular and universal learning need for educators	**Assumes** • Diversity in classroom environments • Multiple and differentiated learning needs for educators

understand this need, collaborative inquiry can be better appreciated as the powerful problem-solving process required to collectively address the adaptive problems they face in improving student learning. This helps to position collaborative inquiry as a viable and preferred solution to the legitimate problem of ineffective professional development.

> "Transforming the culture of a school can be an important enabling condition for teacher leadership" (Spillane, 2006, p. 45).

A caveat must be noted about the terms professional development and professional learning. It is not our intention to polarize these two terms and imply that the call to shift to a professional learning culture negates the occasional need for professional development. One-shot workshops delivered by outside experts are important when there is a need to disseminate knowledge. We caution, however, when districts rely heavily (or solely) on models of professional development. When topics are determined and prioritized by others there is risk of focusing on the "flavor of the month" and introducing content that is irrelevant to the learning needs identified by educators that are directly related to meeting the learning needs of their students. However, if professional development is designed to bridge this gap, it takes on the new purpose of accelerating the learning of educators rather than the stand-alone improvement strategy it has been known as in the past.

Make Explicit the Relationship Between Change and Learning

Learning is personal. Educators can be assured that they have engaged in professional learning when the experience feels personal in such a way that it has impacted their professional identity. An expansion or refinement of an understanding of both student learning and professional learning is embodied in this change. Also embodied in this change is the commitment to learn, lead, and teach differently—a key marker of professional learning. Therefore, the interconnections between change and learning is an important concept to understand in relation to rethinking and reshaping professional identities. Change and learning are concepts existing within a cyclical relationship in which one cannot exist without the other. In other words, true learning demands a change in thinking or behavior, and a need for change necessitates a need for learning. Collaborative inquiry provides the context in which this relationship is observed. Teams engaged in collaborative inquiry create a space in which they normalize or expect and anticipate learning and change to happen.

Initial conversations are aimed to evoke insights and connections to the collaborative inquiry process embodying the nature and relationship between change and learning—being both iterative and adaptive. Table 5.2 provides further clarity to the relationship between change and learning and provides prompts that could be used to guide discussions.

Long-Term Commitment

Making the commitment to shifting from a culture where people were developed to one where practitioners construct their own knowledge requires an adaptive leadership stance. This stance recognizes that shifting culture is a multiyear process. Initial collaborative inquiry cycles are often about orienting teachers to their new role within a professional learning culture. Changing from a culture focused on professional development

Table 5.2 The Relationship Between Change and Learning

Characteristics	Discussion Prompts
Change • Cannot happen without commitment and investment • Recognizes that change is difficult and happens over time with commitment to the end goal (reshaping how we learn)	Consider when you've had to make a personal change (e.g., more time with family, exercise, diet). • Were you successful? • If so, how long did it take you make that change? • How many attempts did you have to take before you found success? • If you have not been successful, what makes it so challenging? • What did or do you have to learn about yourself to make this change?
Learning • Happens when misconceptions are corrected • Misconceptions can be corrected in both the content and process of learning.	When you have made changes in life • What did you have to unlearn? • How did you know you needed to make this change? • What were the types of evidence that told you that you "had it wrong?" • Did you have to change the way you learn to make changes?

to one that is focused on professional learning demands that leaders understand that gains are going to be incremental. Therefore, a long-term investment is required to ensure teacher-driven inquiry is sustained and makes good on its promise to transform learning, leading, and teaching.

Staying the course over the long term also requires that adaptive challenges are continually defined and addressed. Being aware of the six lynchpins described in Chapter 2 provides a starting point in defining challenges. However, over time, as school teams and districts engage in cycles of inquiry, additional adaptive challenges, unique to individual contexts and situations, will likely surface. Adaptive leaders understand that they need to help others navigate through periods of disturbance *and* manage themselves in environments that are likely outside of their zones of comfort (Heifetz et al., 2009). They recognize the importance of pushing forward during times of discomfort, while ensuring individuals are not pushed beyond their limit of tolerance.

Finally, in staying the course, leaders will need to consider *their* beliefs in relation to some of the notions presented in this book. Do facilitators, leaders, and advocates for collaborative inquiry believe

- Engagement should be voluntary?
- Shared leadership is essential?
- That it must be guided through experience (e.g., individuals at every level in the system engage in the process)?
- The complementary nature of collaborative inquiry and school improvement should be capitalized upon?
- Recognition, celebration, and dissemination are vital to the process?
- Facilitation is critical?

To what degree do these beliefs manifest themselves in practice? In other words, to what degree are theories-in-use aligned with espoused theories?

In shaping cultures in which educators advocate for opportunities to engage in high quality learning through inquiry and collaboration, educators must understand the differences between traditional designs and high quality designs. In addition, when traditional designs are delivered, leaders should be transparent as to why. The relationship between change and learning must be made explicit, and a long-term commitment requiring an adaptive leadership stance is needed. Shaping the development of a professional learning culture also requires care and attention to the quality of professional relationships.

BUILDING QUALITY
PROFESSIONAL RELATIONSHIPS

Even though there are many rewards and benefits in utilizing a collaborative inquiry approach to professional learning, there is also a certain amount of ambiguity involved. Collaboratively inquiring into one's practice may seem risky for some. Inherent in the process is the expression of vulnerability as team members share ideas, reveal beliefs, uncover assumptions, expose their practice, and grapple with difficult challenges related to learning, leading, and teaching. Learning and improving become a collaborative and sometimes risky public endeavor.

In professional learning cultures, traditional roles and responsibilities change, and relationships come to be redefined. As classroom teachers are invited to tackle issues related to school improvement, they accept the responsibility for the success of *all* students, not just the ones in their classrooms. As school-based and system leaders are invited to consider issues related to leadership practice, they accept the responsibility of modeling what it is to be a learner. Participants become responsible for creating and sharing knowledge resulting from their inquiries. In addition, we continue to see an evolution in roles as participants at every level in the system are afforded the space to learn and lead. Decisions become less directive in nature and more synergetic in the team's drive toward constant improvement. In several sessions we have been privy to, it is difficult to determine hierarchy amongst participants. Individuals need to be prepared to redefine their roles, take on different responsibilities, step up, and make room, as cultures shift from development minded to learning focused.

The quality of professional relationships is a critical aspect, when considering the conditions necessary to support an approach to school improvement like the one described in this book. In addition to learning about how to increase the success and well-being of students, participants are also learning how to help each other become more effective educators and leaders—which is a complex endeavor. Knight (2011) discussed the complexity of providing support within professional relationships, pointing out that "effective professional learning must be grounded in an understanding of how complex helping relationships can be" (p. 20).

Knight (2011) offered seven Partnership Principles as a way of thinking and being in helping relationships. These ideas can be applied by all team members during a collaborative inquiry cycle to strengthen professional relationships. Since the work of school improvement relies heavily on the quality of professional relationships, educators engaging in collaborative inquiry would benefit from embracing a partnership approach in order to address the complexities of helping adults. Facilitators who embrace and model Knight's (2011) Partnership Principles will help to shape the development of a professional learning culture. The seven Partnership Principles are outlined below.

KNIGHT'S PARTNERSHIP PRINCIPLES APPLIED TO COLLABORATIVE INQUIRY

Principle #1—Equality

The principle of equality can be summed up in the phrase "everyone's ideas and insights matter." During the collaborative inquiry process, team members do not tell each other what to do, they decide together. Knight explained the Partnership Principle of equality in the following sense, "People may bring different skills and knowledge but what's important to note is that everyone deserves to be counted the same—everyone's opinion matters equally" (personal communication, July 21, 2014). Team members build healthier and stronger relationships by listening to one another and accepting each person as an equal—regardless of each person's position within the organization. Embracing everyone as an equal will help reconceptualizing traditional roles and responsibilities (that were often hierarchical in nature) associated with past professional development approaches.

Principle #2—Choice

Knight (2011) argued, "failing to provide real choice in helping relationships is a recipe for disaster" (p. 32) but also noted "meaningful choice can only occur within a structure" (p. 34). Collaborative inquiry provides individuals with the autonomy to determine how they will learn. Once a team identifies the most urgent learning needs of their students, teachers then identify their professional learning needs. How to go about gaining additional knowledge and skills is left up to the participants to choose. Teams often turn to theory, reading research articles and/or engaging in a book study. Sometimes team members opt to observe each other's practice, moderate student work, and/or develop common formative assessments. Allowing participants to determine a structure for learning, based on

> "Conversation can only take place among equals. If anyone feels superior, it destroys conversation. Words are then used to dominate, coerce, manipulate. Those who are superior can't help but treat others as objects to accomplish their causes and plans. If we see each other as equals, we stop misusing them" (Wheatley, 2002, p. 141).

their needs will ensure that participants remain motivated to learn. Relationships are enriched as team members are provided with choice. Educators come to understand professional learning is about their needs and their decisions as professionals.

Principle #3—Voice

In a collaborative inquiry cycle, team members are not told that they must implement step-by-step programs, rather their thoughts and suggestions count. Participants find their voice as they are encouraged (and given freedom) to explore, discover, and develop solutions to the challenges related to their craft. Their voice is honored as they identify, select, test, and evaluate various teaching approaches and strategies. The transformational potential of collaborative inquiry lies in empowering teachers as change agents. Eliciting and respecting teachers' voices is an essential aspect where this is concerned. In addition, relationships are enhanced as team members demonstrate that they value the perspectives of their colleagues.

Principle #4—Reflection

Knight (2011) noted that reflection is only possible when "people have the freedom to accept or reject what they are learning as they see fit" (p. 37). This notion fits nicely within the collaborative inquiry framework, as the process allows educators to dabble with ideas and theories within the context of their unique environments. As outlined in Chapter 4, during reflection, participants consider what worked well for them and what to keep, modify, or discard in light of their individual circumstances. Making room for participants to determine their next steps based on personal reflection is essential to the collaborative inquiry process. When team members are provided the opportunity to engage in deep thinking and provided safe structures for reflecting in a public forum, relationships improve and team members value the process.

Principle #5—Dialogue

Knight (2011) described dialogue as "talking with the goal of digging deeper and exploring ideas together" (p. 38). Since the focus of a team's inquiry is collaboratively determined and shared, dialogue has a greater potential to be rich, focused, and solution-based. The process can move conversations to deeper levels as participants develop common understandings and a shared vocabulary about student learning and leadership and teaching approaches. In applying the principle of dialogue, collaborative inquiry participants are not as concerned with being right as they are with getting things right. Better relationships result when dialogue is focused on what is best for students rather than whose way is best.

Principle #6—Praxis

Praxis is about applying learning to real-life practice. "Praxis is enabled when teachers have a chance to explore, prod, stretch, and re-create whatever it is they are studying—to roll up their sleeves, really consider how they teach, really learn a new approach, and then reconsider their teaching practice and reshape the new approach" (Knight, 2011, p. 43). The principle of praxis describes what takes place during a collaborative inquiry cycle. Coupled with reflection, participants implement new and different approaches in their practice in order to determine how to meet the learning needs of their audience. Educators explore and modify approaches accordingly. As they test strategies and determine how to adapt them, they are engaging in praxis. The connection to real-life practice is essential in shifting from a culture of development to a culture of learning.

Principle #7—Reciprocity

The essence of this principle is that we should expect as much as we give. Collaborative inquiry requires participants to interrogate classroom and leadership practices that have been traditionally private while assuming the role of a learner. Through the sharing of practices, individuals abandon a knowing stance and adopt a learning stance. Applying the principle of reciprocity means that we can truly expect to learn with and from each other. Team members build healthier and stronger relationships by expecting to get from their colleagues as much as they give to them.

THE ROLE OF TRUST

In addition to considering Knight's (2011) Partnership Principles when building quality relationships, trust must be considered, as it is the bedrock of all relationships. Trust provides a foundation for meaningful discussion and is a key component in shaping the development of cultures of professional learning. Without trust, team members will have a more difficult time examining and self-correcting long-standing misconceptions and assumptions underlying the adaptive problems they have identified.

Our operating definition of trust is a willingness to take risks and to be vulnerable with others. Trust in a collaborative inquiry team involves a willingness to expose problems of practice, self-identifying lack of common understandings, asking questions (even if we think they are inane), granting permission to others to teach you, and trying new approaches. We recently worked with a team of five middle school teachers and witnessed a conversation where trust was readily apparent. Their shared problem of practice involved supporting greater self-regulation in students. As each shared their working definition of self-regulation, they acknowledged they were uncertain and lacked confidence in their understanding of the term. Team members admitted not knowing how to foster self-regulation in their students and asked questions in an effort to learn from each other. From our perspective, each member of the team was willing to take a risk and be vulnerable.

It is often assumed that one needs to work actively to establish trusting environments where people are willing to take risks and share their vulnerability. Tschannen-Moran (2013), however, noted that the "wariness of distrust takes a lot of energy" (p. 4), and so in the absence of any warning signs, provisional trust is readily extended because it is an easier option. Trust, however, can be lost if not maintained. In the example above, if a team member was perceived as judgmental or all knowing, trust may have broken down. Leaders and facilitators must not take for granted this reality if a teacher-driven inquiry culture is to be established.

> "Trust is more of a product of collaborative encounters than a prerequisite for them" (Katz & Dack, 2013, p. 92).

In their research on trust, Schoorman, Mayer, and Davis (2007) argued that "trust is an aspect of relationships" (p. 344) and suggested that trust is maintained based on people's perceptions of three major drivers. These include ability, benevolence, and integrity. Perceived ability is situation specific—is the person able to do what they say they can do? Perceived benevolence establishes that the person cares and that his or her motivations are not related to ego or self-gratification. Tschannen-Moran (2013) described benevolence as "whether or not there is a sense of mutual good" (p. 5). Finally, integrity involves living with a set of values that others agree with.

Tschannen-Moran (2013) noted that trust can be taught and learned and suggested that leaders take the time to build quality relationships by demonstrating "genuine caring and a sense of benevolence about people as human beings, not just as functionaries in the organization" (p. 6). In order to build and maintain trust, facilitators of collaborative inquiry teams consider the following questions:

- Are every one's interests taken into account?
- Have all voices been heard?
- Are decisions shared by the team?
- Is there transparency about reasons why decisions are made?
- Are equity and student achievement at the forefront of what we do?
- What risks are involved? How can risk be minimized?
- What commitments do we need to make and follow through before we meet again?

Without the establishment and maintenance of trust as part of the shift in culture, teacher teams may resist engaging in the depth of discussion needed to critically assess the impact of their actions. In addition, embracing Knight's (2011) Partnership Principles will help in developing the quality professional relationships that are necessary for this work to flourish.

> "The need for a climate of trust in the staffroom is obvious if the profession is to be based on collaboration" (Hattie, 2015, p. 24).

IMPROVING COLLABORATION

Facilitators of collaborative inquiry play an important role in shifting cultures, because they help to fundamentally change the way teachers learn together. As teams cycle through the process, they not only improve their practice but they also improve the way they learn. Teams rely on the collaborative power of the group (social capital) to ensure adaptive challenges are overcome. As individuals engage in collaborative inquiry, they are constantly negotiating and renegotiating what collaboration means and what it can result in. Developing the team's social capital—their ability to draw on their collaborative power—requires thoughtfulness and attention on the part of the facilitator.

Understanding how effective teams operate and developing their capacity to improve is an important aspect in leading collaborative inquiry. Facilitators use knowledge and skills related to various areas, including decision-making and problem-solving, managing professional-learning sessions, effective communication, and interpersonal and intrapersonal development, in order to improve collaboration. Facilitators also use knowledge of various stances individuals

> Throughout this book, we have argued that through engagement in collaborative inquiry, professional practice is reconstructed—whether it is leadership practice or instructional practice. We also encourage facilitators to consider the practice of facilitation and, in particular, how to improve the quality of collaboration within teams.

take in determining to what degree they will invest in the group in order to cocreate norms and further develop the team. In addition, by understanding the role of conflict and helping educators manage it, collaboration is improved.

> "Professionals understand the power of the team, promote the development of the team, and become integral parts of the team themselves" (Hargreaves & Fullan, 2012, p. 23).

Developing the Team

Table 5.3 outlines the knowledge and skills that we have continuously drawn upon to develop teams. Facilitators could use this list in order to assess their strengths and identify areas of focus for themselves and the teams they lead.

Table 5.3 Facilitator Knowledge and Skills for Team Development

Area	Specific Knowledge and Skills
Decision-making and problem-solving	• Build consensus. • Identify the drivers and factors that contribute to an identified problem. • Provide clarity on the factors that the group has influence over. • Integrate points of disagreement to see if a stronger solution can be created.
Meeting management	• Know when to discuss versus decide. • Monitor time to ensure appropriate amounts are spent on discussion. • Transition from one component of a meeting to another. • Review outcomes and next steps at the conclusion of meetings.
Effective communication	• Monitor non-verbal signals and messages. • Redirect or reorient discussions that are not productive. • Rephrase key points that drive discussions and decisions forward.
Reflection for inter- and intrapersonal development	• Ensure all perspectives in the group are heard and understood. • Articulate underlying personal assumptions and biases that members may not have awareness of.

Improving Outcomes for English Language Learners

Focusing on improving outcomes for English language learners (ELLs), Gillian Hall, education officer with Ontario's Ministry of Education, facilitates professional learning facilitators' (PLF) collaborative inquiries. Gillian along with her colleagues at the ministry recognized that professional learning facilitators required support in making the transition from being presenters of knowledge to becoming facilitators of teachers' learning. They established networks of PLFs from different school districts. These networks met five times during the year to debrief the experiences they were having leading collaborative inquiry in their districts and learn about various leadership techniques along with different aspects of collaborative inquiry.

Gillian works to support these PLFs and has witnessed the transformative power in the design, noting the teachers the PLF's work with have made permanent changes to their practice and reconstructed beliefs about the best ways to support ELLs. The key difference noted is that the teachers own their learning and their actions; collaborative inquiry provided an authentic opportunity to reflect upon their learning and actions in a safe environment. In one school, a collaborative inquiry team's vision and mission of improving experiences of ELLs transferred to an entire faculty and resulted in the creation of a more inclusive school environment.

In addition to refining knowledge and skills related to facilitation, it is helpful to understand factors that contribute to an individual's investment on a team. Team development is highly dependent on individuals' personal choices, which are contingent on the stance he or she assumes, driven by personal questions, and characterized by interactions with others. The team development model outlined in Table 5.4 highlights the stances individuals take in determining to what degree they will invest in the group. The individual stances are not to be mistaken as stages that one evolves through over time; instead they determine whether a team will actually form and the degree of collaboration that can be expected. In each stage of collaborative inquiry, individuals may find themselves vacillating between different stances as they learn how to capitalize on the collaborative power of the team and redefine notions of powerful professional learning.

> In a study by Given et al. (2010), the facilitator used her own documentation of the teacher meetings to analyze the evolving-democratic processes of the inquiry group. Facilitators might consider ways to document collaborative inquiry team meetings in order to study collaboration and improve facilitation.

Table 5.4 Individual Stances Determining Team Investment

Individual Stances	Individuals Seek to Answer . . .	Interactions Characterized by . . .	Collaboration Characterized by . . .
Civility	Who I am grouped with? What is important to each person in this group? What do I feel comfortable revealing about myself? Am I compatible with people in this group?	Courteous and polite behavior Protective of personal thoughts	Sharing of successful strategies Reassurances Superficial levels of discourse
Convergence	How can being part of this group benefit me? To what degree do my needs and desires conflict with others? How will we work together? What will the work be?	Monitoring of adherence to established and agreed upon norms Expectation that personal needs and desires are understood but not necessarily explicitly stated	Common critical issues uncovered Exploration of broader implications Curiosity modeled
Clash	How will we disagree? Do I feel safe to disagree? What will others think of me if I disagree? Can we still be kind but critical?	Potential passive aggressive behaviors Marked withdrawal when engagement was previously high	Dismissal—waste of time attitudes Blame deflected to factors outside one's control rather than deep analysis of practice
Commitment	Am I assured that we place value in one another? What are the ways I can let others know that I value them? Is changing my mind okay?	Candor that does not threaten but encourages critical thinking Personal responsibility becomes synonymous with accountability	Shared decision-making Public and collective questioning and reflection on practice Shared responsibility for leading, learning, and teaching Focus on impact

Foundational to this model of team development are key understandings and approaches facilitators take in regard to establishing and maintaining team norms and trust. Trust was addressed in the previous discussion regarding building quality professional relationships. Developing norms for interactions are considered in the section that follows.

> "We need a different set of interpersonal skills that create collective inquiry so that we can learn from our experiences together and develop common understandings" (Bushe, 2010, p. 261).

Cocreating Norms for Interactions

Norms are understood as the team's agreements for interpersonal interactions. These agreements are initially explicit and verbalized but eventually become cultural (unsaid but understood) expectations of how individuals on the team should conduct themselves. These norms are initially established to increase human and social capital by encouraging individual behaviors that contribute to team efficiency while simultaneously deterring behaviors that derail effective collaboration.

Nelson, Perkins, and Hathorn (2008) found that the "intentional attention to the co-construction and maintenance of collaborative norms" enabled collaborative inquiry team's ability to function (p. 1298) and that norms provided for "trust amongst group members which made talking about one's beliefs about teaching and learning safe to do (p. 1291). The explicit acceptance of collaborative norms also allowed the team to invoke the norms when tensions emerged. "This agreed upon avenue for dialogue" (p. 1291) enabled the team to maintain an inquiry stance.

Lipton and Wellman (2011) suggested that facilitators structure collaborative work bearing in mind dynamic tensions that individuals face in group work. Each tension is described along a continuum and aligned to the utilization of time and how successful work is defined and completed. Three of the tensions include (a) task versus relationship; (b) certainty versus ambiguity; and (c) detail versus big picture. When these tensions are not recognized, valued, and addressed by the team, individuals may unintentionally sabotage any potential for high quality collaboration. We have found the tensions to be an ideal framework for the cocreation of norms. Table 5.5 highlights the key features of each tension and sample norms that strike a balance within each tension.

The purpose is to create norms that encourage a stance toward commitment (outlined in the bottom row of Table 5.4) characterized by interactions in which candor encourages critical thinking and personal responsibility becomes synonymous with accountability. Ultimately, the aim is for collaboration characterized by shared decision-making; public and collective questioning and reflection on practice; shared responsibility for learning, leading, and teaching; and a focus on individual and collective impact. The sample norms outlined in Table 5.5 are closely aligned with the questions posed earlier in relation to building and maintaining trust. When facilitators carefully and collaboratively craft norms related to the three tensions outlined by Lipton and Wellman (2011), teams' perceptions of the three major drivers of trust (ability, benevolence, and integrity) become more solidified.

Table 5.5   Dynamic Tensions: A Framework for the Cocreation of Norms

Dynamic Tension	Description	Sample Norms
Task–Relationship	Underscores socioemotional nature of collaboration. When working together, individuals may perceive that work is overvalued, especially when the development of interpersonal connections is sacrificed. For these individuals, relationships are just as valuable as the completion of a task itself.	We take time to "check in" with everyone. We stay focused on what we need to accomplish.
Certainty–Ambiguity	Characterized by the level of tolerance individuals have for clarity or vagueness about next steps and actions for the group. If steps are too narrowly defined and don't provide flexibility for responsiveness or choice, individuals may discredit the effort and disengage.	We will end each meeting being clear on what our next steps are. We will take time to ask after every completed step whether something needs to be adjusted or reconsidered.
Detail–Big Picture	Highlights individual preferences for the shaping of collective work. For some individuals, energy and commitment is generated when specifics regarding how work will be completed are determined. For others, energy and commitment is generated when the group's work is clearly positioned as part of a larger and systemic goal.	We will ensure that everyone understands how we will systematically get the work done. We will be clear about the more global goal we are trying to reach by doing this work.

Establishment of norms are foundational to improving collaboration, since they identify and explicitly name what individuals need and value when working in teams. The creation of norms does not guarantee, however, that conflict will not arise. When individuals have different points of view, differences sometimes escalate to conflict. How conflict is handled determines whether it works to a collaborative inquiry team's advantage or contributes to its demise. Beginning with creating safety both within individuals and teams for struggle to take place, facilitators help educators navigate conflict so that they develop an appreciation for the growth that only comes from addressing differences in opinions.

Navigating Conflict

Facilitators must be equipped to help participants of collaborative inquiry position conflict as an indicator of success and not a fault in the collaborative inquiry process itself. Understanding the role of conflict and helping educators manage it results in opportunities for learning and change. Recognizing the value of cognitive conflict is a way for teams to gain deeper understandings about the complexities of learning, leading, and teaching.

Achinstein (2002) sought to understand the role of conflict in sustaining learning communities over time and demonstrated how the vastly different ways in which communities navigated disagreements impacted their capacity for organizational learning.

Communities either avoided or embraced conflict. When communities embraced conflict, they had "greater potential for continual growth and renewal" (p. 448). Achinstein (2002) noted that embracing conflict involved acknowledging, soliciting, and owning conflict

"Disagreement is more frequent in schools with collaborative cultures because purposes, values, and their relationship to practice are always up for discussion. But this disagreement is made possible by the bedrock of fundamental security on which staff relationships rest—in the knowledge that open discussions and temporary disagreements will not threaten continuing relationships" (Hargreaves & Fullan, 2012, p. 113).

"Conflicts cannot simply be ignored and repressed by force of authority. Instead, what's required in an ability to get things out in the open and clear the air, to build real commitment to decisions, to develop synergistic teams, and to be able to openly discuss failures and successes and learn from everyone's experience" (Bushe, 2010, p. 261).

Earl and Katz's (2007) research identified the importance of moderate professional conflict as a key enabler of a professional learning culture that impacts student achievement.

by "critically reflecting upon differences of belief and practice" (p. 441). The author suggested that mechanisms for openly raising and addressing conflicts be put in place.

Ways to critically reflect upon differences in beliefs and practice were suggested in Chapter 4. The Reflecting on Practice template (Resource B) and Reflecting on Theories of Action template (Resource C) are mechanisms likely to raise conflicts as individuals' differences in beliefs and philosophies are uncovered. In order to address conflict, Garmston (2012) noted the importance of distinguishing between cognitive conflict and affective conflict. Affective conflict focuses "on personalized anger or resentment, usually directed at individuals rather than ideas" (p. 107). Cognitive conflict focuses attention "on the all-too-often ignored assumptions that may underlie a particular issue" (p. 107). The aim is to use cognitive conflict productively by engaging in cognitive disagreements without personalizing them.

Facilitators guide collaborative inquiry teams in separating *person* from *practice* by focusing on the problem, not individuals. Referring to norms and/or group-generated sets of questions (described in Chapter 4) are helpful strategies. Operating from Knight's (2011) Partnership Principles is also important. Revisiting assumptions contained in theories of action, positive paraphrasing, and well-crafted questions are also ways to use cognitive conflict productively.

Bushe (2012) suggested that confronting for insight helps to bring up difficult issues without diminishing an individual. Confronting for insight is about extending an invitation to help better understand someone's experience and, when done successfully, results in increased awareness while enhancing the quality of the relationship. It involves sharing observations—void inferences made about the observations. City et al. (2009) also suggested starting with observation at the descriptive level—"without heavy judgemental overlay that we typically bring" (p. 87). The authors noted that, while it is difficult to stay in the descriptive mode, it is critical, because descriptive statements provide a common basis for conversation. By describing our observations, it helps "open the door to conversation rather than close it" (City et al., 2009, p. 92).

When facilitators build their knowledge and skills and reflect on the practice of facilitation, team member's experiences are enhanced. Utilizing knowledge about individual stances and coconstructing norms for interaction help in developing collaborative inquiry teams. In addition, recognizing the differences between cognitive and affective conflict and confronting for insight helps to navigate conflict in ways that are productive to the team.

EXPANDING THE REACH OF LEARNING

Expanding the reach of learning involves recognizing and celebrating individuals and teams for their efforts. Through celebration, efforts are acknowledged and team members become increasingly motivated to engage in the next cycle of inquiry. By engaging teams in celebration, teams' collective efforts are honored and collaborative inquiry is reinforced as an empowering approach for considering the impact of educator actions on student outcomes. Collective efficacy is also reinforced when teams celebrate what they were able to accomplish together.

> Celebrations signal what is important and reinforce shared values (DuFour, 1998).

Expanding the reach of learning also involves documenting and disseminating knowledge that was gained throughout the process. Documenting the work is an important part of the process, because it helps teams articulate and clarify thoughts. Teams use documentation to identify strengths, ideas, and next steps to support learning. Sharing experiences about how the team worked through an educational concern will help others in recognizing the benefits of engaging in the process. Therefore, it is also important to create opportunities for knowledge to be disseminated. By identifying recognition and dissemination as a lynchpin (Chapter 2) vital to ensuring collaborative inquiry reaches scale, we hoped to underscore their importance. Collaborative inquiry as a means of changing practice is much more likely to reach scale when educators witness it, either firsthand or vicariously through their colleagues. Good ideas in education spread exponentially when enough individuals enthusiastically share their positive-learning experiences with others, wanting them to have the same experience. They approach this sharing with such conviction, others willingly try it out themselves, have a similarly positive experience, and the cycle of sharing repeats itself. Five strategies to expand the reach of learning are offered in the section that follows.

> Given et al. (2010) noted that "documentation means more than a collection of teacher- or student-produced artifacts; it includes the conversations and reflections such artifacts evoke" (p. 38).

STRATEGIES TO EXPAND THE REACH OF LEARNING

Establish Networks

Networks are formed for the purpose of sharing ideas and resources and allow individuals and teams to gain additional perspectives and

Rincon-Gallardo and Fullan (2016) listed "continuously improving practice and systems through cycles of collaborative inquiry" as one of eight essential features of effective networks.

insights, beyond their schools or school districts, into their professional practice. Katz et al. (2009) noted that "professional networks, increasingly are being promoted as mechanisms to intentionally create the level of deep learning necessary for practitioners that can lever the kinds of changes that make a difference for students" (p. 2). Through collaborative inquiry, teams discover what works (or what does not work) and, although the results are contextually relevant, there is a lot to be learned from teams' conclusions and recommendations. Networks provide a venue for sharing and engaging in dialogue and, as a result, collaborative inquiry teams gain additional insights in regard to solving adaptive challenges.

"The most effective central office administrators will become the architects of networks in which effective instructional practice is shared in as few degrees of separation as possible" (Reeves, 2008, p. 81).

Networks also provide opportunities for educators to study and learn more about facilitating collaborative inquiry. We have lead and participated in networks in Ontario designed for leaders of school and system learning. Facilitators come together to consider how to enact their practice skillfully, be observed and observe others in practice, obtain feedback, and share reflections. As participants consider how to strengthen various aspects in regard to supporting collaborative inquiry cycles, they often find they share similar challenges at similar points in time. Learning is strengthened as individuals work to solve facilitation challenges together.

Hargreaves and Fullan (2012) noted that "enabling teachers to learn from each other within and across schools—and building cultures and networks of communication, learning, trust, and collaboration" (p. 89) was one of the most powerful strategies in all of education. Furthermore, findings indicate that "well-connected teacher networks were associated with strong teacher collective efficacy, which in turn supported student achievement" (Moolenaar et al., 2012, p. 251). The reach of learning can be expanded through the establishment of networks.

Create Online Spaces for Collaboration

While face-to-face communication is important, there are benefits to setting up online spaces for inquiry teams to collaborate as well. When time and distance are a challenge, teams can connect online and collaborate synchronously or asynchronously. Online spaces also provide an opportunity to archive learning. Some collaborative inquiry teams archive their learning using Google Docs. The Revision History enables teams to review the history of changes (changes in thinking) that occurred throughout the process. The documents created by teams not only provide evidence of changes in thinking and behavior, they provide a valuable historical context for participants joining existing teams. Recently, one of us witnessed a case in which a team's Google Doc eased a new teacher's entry into the process and fostered further reflection by team members. Questions arose for the new teacher as she reviewed the team's current and revised thinking. Posing the questions to the existing team resulted in deeper reflection and the need to further consider the reasons behind their past and present actions. Most school districts have online spaces that can easily be accessed and utilized for collaborative work.

Making Learning Visible at the Simcoe County District School Board

The Simcoe County District School Board in Ontario, Canada, is utilizing an online environment to deepen learning and increase collaboration within and among inquiry teams. Teams are invited to share their "Learning Stories" using an online template that prompts team members to reflect during each phase in the collaborative inquiry cycle. Participants articulate their learning and next steps, making their thinking visible to others. Recognizing the importance of learning by doing, the principal of innovation, Patrick Miller, and the principal of program, Dean Maltby, noted that administrators engage in collaborative inquiry and share their Learning Stories as well (personal communication, November 5, 2015).

Miller credited Superintendent Anita Simpson for setting up the conditions for this work to be possible. Miller explained that "It's not about surveillance for us. That usually leads to compliance. There is a focus on local and system moderation of collaborative inquiries as well as monitoring. We are working toward commitment" (personal communication, November 5, 2015). In order to move from compliance to commitment the following questions are considered:

- Does it foster a culture of learning?
- Does it promote voice and choice?
- Does it support professional development through inquiry?
- Does it leverage digital tools and resources?
- Does it contribute to a growth mindset?
- Does it nurture a culture of collaboration?
- Does it allow for modeling from the classroom to the boardroom?

(Continued)

(Continued)

Every team's Learning Story is accessible to every education in the district. Reflecting and sharing online has not only helped in mobilizing knowledge gained through collaborative inquiries, it has broadened networks and resources available to teams. It also enables principals to more closely monitor team's progress, provide precise support, and engage in more meaningful conversations. As principals can easily access information about what teachers are inquiring and learning about, it helps them in assisting teams in more meaningful ways throughout each stage in the cycle. In addition, administrators collaboratively learn more about how to support teams by examining and asking questions about the Learning Stories in each other's schools during their monthly meetings.

The student-learning needs identified through collaborative inquiries inform the School's Learning Plan (formally known as the School Improvement Plan), which in turn, informs the District's Learning Plan. Furthermore, the collection of Learning Stories provide documentation of organizational learning that can later be analyzed for purposes of accountability and informing district-wide theories of action.

Host a Learning Fair

During a learning fair, teams share what they have learned, along with their successes and challenges while engaging in the process. By structuring sharing under two tracks: (1) Learning about Professional Learning and Leadership and (2) Learning about Student Learning, teams have the opportunity to reflect on both educator and student learning that resulted from their inquiry. Teams visiting the fair can listen for information that can help them accelerate their own inquiries. Learning fairs provide an optimum opportunity for school and system leaders to gather evidence of organizational learning. Records of inquiry questions posed, theories of action, and reflections provide a rich source of evidence that can be gathered and examined year-to-year in order to document progress throughout a system. It is important to note that the purpose of this type of sharing is to foster cooperation—not competition—and should be designed as such. We have witnessed very creative ways that teams have documented their journey, including timelines, scrapbooks, three-panel display boards, videos, and journals. Particularly powerful displays include student voices.

Given et al. (2010) noted that the "tools used to make teaching and learning visible to colleagues are also vital to the instructional change process" (p. 37).

Host a Facilitator Summit

Facilitators of collaborative inquiry are developing a set of leadership skills that need constant reflection, so that facilitative approaches can be refined and used with more precision. A summit for facilitators could be a forum in which facilitators share their best practices, as it relates to how they help guide inquiries and shape teams. The focus of the summit would highlight ways that facilitators assess where individuals are in their commitments to developing a team, cocreating team developing norms, steering teams through times of conflict, and how to skillfully listen and respond to team members to amplify conversations that generate critical thinking and reflection. Facilitators could bring protocols and tools to share their developing leadership practice.

Encourage Publication and Opportunities for Presentations

Collaborative inquiry has the unique and privileged position of occurring in the context of the classroom. This position allows teachers to experiment with research-based instructional approaches in their classrooms and tailor them to the needs of individual students. Lessons learned from diversity in application could be used by others. Schools and districts could create online newsletters that highlight how inquiry teams are tailoring researched practices into their classrooms. Teams could also be encouraged to submit their learning to teacher federation publications and subject specific associations to broaden the reach of their learning.

As suggested previously, professional development is an important part of effective professional learning. What teacher teams have learned and applied in their classrooms might be the expert knowledge that other inquiry teams are looking for. If school districts create databases where the results of inquiries are shared, then other teams could use the databases to find teachers who could come and present to their findings to them. This cycle of one team's professional learning grounding the professional development of another team is an indicator of the shift in learning culture advocated for in this book. Other opportunities for teams to share their learning could be at conferences hosted by professional associations or in emerging alternative conferences like Open Space or EdCamp.

Fisher et al. (2012) noted that the "culture of a school is not something that can be left to chance, nor can it be seen as something beyond our control" (p. 15). Facilitators can help to shape the development of a professional learning culture where individuals and teams value collaboration, embrace transparency, persist through times of challenge, and recognize what can be accomplished collectively. Ideas contained in this chapter included unpacking the differences between professional development and professional learning, building quality relationships, improving collaboration by developing the team and analyzing team processes, establishing and maintaining trust, and skillfully navigating conflict.

The facilitator's aim is to create powerful and positive first experiences with collaborative inquiry to the extent that teachers demand more of these experiences—the driving force behind the shift to a professional learning culture. When value and importance is placed on the process of learning, teachers embrace the process and ultimately become agents in shifting from cultures of development to cultures of learning. This shift ensures that future iterations of collaborative inquiry cycles can continue to meet the target of changing practice and improving learning for both educators and students.

Reeves (2010) noted that it "is not the case that we need a new theory of effective professional learning; what we need is a practical mechanism to turn our ideas into reality" (p. 23). Collaborative inquiry is the practical mechanism that is needed. It is a way to achieve Coburn's (2003) redefined notion of scale. Supporting a wider and deeper adoption of collaborative inquiry includes being aware of the lynchpins, identifying adaptive challenges, and skillful facilitation. Collaborative inquiry is characterized by a willingness to investigate learning, leading, and teaching connections. Educators develop professional capital by surfacing their own biases in regard to pedagogy and student learning. Teachers must continually challenge current practices and embrace the idea that failures and missteps are necessary for continuous improvement and not a reflection of effort or ability. Facilitators play a critical role in creating the conditions in which these important conversations take place.

Facilitators support teams in establishing and maintaining a needs-based focus, so that teams invest in what matters the most. Collaborative inquiry teams identify student-learning needs, develop questions they are genuinely curious about, formulate a robust theory of action, and identify assumptions. Facilitators also support teams by provoking thinking necessary to assess impact so that educators have a clear understanding of how their actions impact student outcomes. This includes building educators' capacities to use assessment data, collaboratively analyzing student work, reconciling discrepancies in theories of action, and determining the next best move. Finally, facilitators help shape the development of a professional learning culture so that inquiry and collaboration become a habit of mind. Consideration of the influence culture has in the adoption of collaborative inquiry is incredibly important. Leaders and facilitators cannot undervalue the important work of shifting cultures to ensure that the roots of collaborative inquiry can grow deep.

Building quality professional relationships, shifting from cultures defined by professional development to one focused on professional learning, improving collaboration, and expanding the reach of learning are important concepts when considering shaping the development of a professional learning culture.

Collaborative inquiry holds the potential to transform school systems into learning organizations. In order to meet students' learning needs and overcome adaptive challenges, teachers, school leaders, and system leaders must have mechanisms and processes in place to collaboratively identify how schools should improve and how to meaningfully refine and sustain those changes. Collaborative inquiry holds the potential to do that by calling educators to raise within themselves a truer sense of learner and leader. As it is teacher-centered, teachers have the power to shape, lead, and take responsibility for learning opportunities, and thus it results in greater ownership of school improvement. If given the time and space and provided the opportunity to identify and solve problems of practice together, innovation will occur and the work will be self-sustaining.

One final note related to the Cardworks depicting our theories of action that introduced each chapter in this book. Bushe (2010) suggested that "helping another person make a card usually leads both parties to develop a much deeper insight into their maps and contributes to good working relationships" (p. 167). This was true for us in developing our cards and we encourage readers to create their own cards and help others in doing so as well.

Resource A

Questions to Strengthen Evidence Collection

QUESTIONS TO CONSIDER IN REGARD TO THE COLLECTION OF STUDENT-LEARNING DATA

- Do team members share a common understanding of the student-learning need that has been identified?
- What would the student-learning evidence look like if students were performing at the highest level? Lowest level? Somewhere in between?
- Does the evidence measure student learning or is it measuring something else?
- What are different ways to collect evidence that could reflect potential changes in student learning over time?
- How and when will team members collect student-learning data?
- Is evidence formative or summative in nature? Does this matter? If so, why?

QUESTIONS TO CONSIDER IN REGARD TO THE COLLECTION OF DEMOGRAPHIC DATA

- Which groups of students do teams need to carefully consider given the identified student learning need?

- Does the collaborative inquiry team know which groups of students are high performing? Low performing? At-risk? If not, how can the team find out?

QUESTIONS TO CONSIDER IN REGARD TO THE COLLECTION OF SCHOOL PROCESS DATA

- What school processes (most likely classroom practices) are collaborative inquiry teams identifying as a means to address gaps in student learning?
- How does this new practice differ from a teacher's regular practice? (Is it really a change?)
- Is there a research base to support the new practice?
- Do team members share a common understanding of new instructional approaches?
- What additional knowledge and skills do educators need in order to implement new approaches?
- How will you know the new practice was implemented?
- How will you know to what level it was implemented?
- What supports do teachers need to "stay the course" (given it is the "right" course)?

QUESTIONS TO CONSIDER IN REGARD TO THE COLLECTION OF PERCEPTUAL DATA

- Does the team's inquiry require the collection of perceptions? If so, whose?
- How will the collection of perceptual data help the team answer its question?
- If collected, what is this information going to tell us? How will it help advance the work of the team?

Resource B

Reflecting on Practice

Individual	Collective
What was different from my regular practice?	What elements were the same as what we do in our practice?
What went well?	Why did it go well?
What did not go well?	Why did it not go well?
What have I learned?	What lessons can we take away from this that will inform our practice?
What (if anything) will I permanently change in my practice?	What (if anything) will we permanently change in our practice?

Resource C

Reflecting on Theories of Action

What is the ideal?	What is real?
What was expected?	What occurred?
What actions were taken?	What were the reasons for the action?
What are alternative strategies?	What is the next best move?
What new assumptions are arising?	What do we need to learn more about?

Resource D

Identifying the Gap: Practice and Values Assessment *for* Learning

Scale X
The School Now
The Classroom Now
(About Your Practice)

Scale Y
How important are your assessment practices for creating opportunities for students to learn?
(About Your Values)

Never true	Rarely true	Often true	Mostly true	Assessment *for* Learning	Not important at all	Of limited importance	Important	Crucial	Bad practice
Never true	Rarely true	Often true	Mostly true	1. Explicitly sharing learning intentions and success criteria so that they could be used as a point of reference for feedback	Not important at all	Of limited importance	Important	Crucial	Bad practice
Never true	Rarely true	Often true	Mostly true	2. Encouraging students to make judgments about the quality of work, based on success criteria, during its actual production	Not important at all	Of limited importance	Important	Crucial	Bad practice
Never true	Rarely true	Often true	Mostly true	3. Enabling students to compare their actual level of achievement with an expected standard	Not important at all	Of limited importance	Important	Crucial	Bad practice
Never true	Rarely true	Often true	Mostly true	4. Increasing students' ability to self-monitor as an important component of the feedback process	Not important at all	Of limited importance	Important	Crucial	Bad practice
Never true	Rarely true	Often true	Mostly true	5. Creating opportunities throughout lessons to discuss with students ways of improving learning how to learn	Not important at all	Of limited importance	Important	Crucial	Bad practice
Never true	Rarely true	Often true	Mostly true	6. Involving students in important decisions shaping their learning, such as planning, monitoring, and evaluating their learning	Not important at all	Of limited importance	Important	Crucial	Bad practice
Never true	Rarely true	Often true	Mostly true	7. Providing students with opportunities to assess each other's work and learning	Not important at all	Of limited importance	Important	Crucial	Bad practice
Never true	Rarely true	Often true	Mostly true	8. Providing descriptive feedback that helps the students articulate (in relation to the learning intentions and success criteria): Where am I going? How am I going? Where to next?	Not important at all	Of limited importance	Important	Crucial	Bad practice

References

Achinstein, B. (2002). Conflict amid community: The micropolitics of teacher collaboration. *Teachers College Record, 104*(3), 421–455.

Argyris, C., & Schön, D. (1978). *Organizational learning: A theory of action perspective.* Addison Wesley: Boston, MA.

Ball, D., & Cohen, D. (1999). Developing practice, developing practitioners: Toward a practice-based theory of professional education. In G. Sykes and L. Darling-Hammond (Eds.), *Teaching as the learning profession: Handbook of policy and practice* (3–32). Jossey Bass: San Francisco, CA.

Bandura, A. (1997). *Self-efficacy: The exercise of control.* W. H. Freeman: New York, NY.

Beauchamp, L., Klassen, R., Parsons, J., Durksen, T., & Taylor, L. (2014). *Exploring the development of teacher efficacy through professional learning experiences.* Alberta Teachers' Association.

Bernhardt, V. (2000). Intersections: New routes open when one type of data crosses another. *Journal of Staff Development, 21*(1), 33–36.

BCG Consulting. (2014). *Teachers know best: Teachers' views on professional development.* Bill & Melinda Gates Foundation.

Bransford, J., Brown, A., & Cocking, R. (2000). *How people learn: Brain, mind, experience, and school* (exp. ed.). National Academy Press: Washington, D.C.

Bruce, C., & Flynn, T. (2013). Assessing the effects of collaborative professional learning: Efficacy shifts in a three-year mathematics study. *Alberta Journal of Educational Research, 58*(4), 691–709.

Bryk, A., Gomez, L., Grunow, A., & LeMahieu, P. (2015). *Learning to improve: How America's schools can get better at getting better.* Harvard Education Press: Cambridge, MA.

Bushe, G. (2010). *Clear leadership: Sustaining real collaboration and partnership at work* (revised ed.). Davis Black: Boston, MA.

Bushe, G., & Marshak, R. (Eds.). (2015). *Dialogic organization development: The theory and practice of transformational change.* Berrett-Koehler: Oakland, CA.

City, E., Elmore, R., Fiarman, S., & Teitel, L. (2009). *Instructional rounds in education: A network approach to improving teaching and learning.* Harvard Education Press: Cambridge, MA.

Coburn, C. (2003). Rethinking scale: Moving beyond numbers to deep and lasting change. *Education Researcher, 32*(6), 3–12.

Colton, A., Langer, G., & Goff, L. (2016). *The collaborative analysis of student learning: Professional learning that promotes success for all.* Corwin: Thousand Oaks, CA.

Cooper-Twamley, S. (2009). *Action research and its impact on teacher efficacy: A mixed methods case study* (Unpublished dissertation). Baylor University.

Copland, M. (2003). Leadership of inquiry: Building and sustaining capacity for school improvement. *Educational Evaluation and Policy Analysis, 25*(4), 375–395.

Csikszentmihalyi, M. (1990). *Flow: The psychology of optimal experience.* Harper Collins: New York, NY.

Darling-Hammond, L. (1998). Teacher learning that supports student learning. *Educational Leadership, 55*(5), 6–11.

Darling-Hammond, Orcutt, Strobel, Kirsch, Lit, & Martin. (n.d.). *Feelings count: Emotions and learning. Theory into practice series.* [Episode 5]. Retrieved from Stanford University School of Education http://www.learner.org/resources/series172.html.

Derrington, M., & Angelle, P. (2013). Teacher leadership and collective efficacy: Connections and links. *International Journal of Teacher Leadership, 4*(1), p. 1–13.

DuFour, R. (1998). Why celebrate? It sends a vivid message about what is valued. *Journal of Staff Development, 19*(4), 58–59.

Dweck, C. (2006). *Mindset: A new psychology of success.* Random House: New York, NY.

Earl, L., & Katz, S. (2007). Leadership in networked learning communities: Defining the terrain. *School Leadership and Management, 27*(3), 239–258.

Eells, R. (2011). *Meta-analysis of the relationship between collective efficacy and student achievement* (Unpublished doctoral dissertation). Loyola University of Chicago.

Elmore, R. (2008). *School reform from the inside out: Policy, practice, and performance.* Harvard Education Press: Cambridge, MA.

Emihovich, C., & Battaglia, C. (2000). Creating cultures for collaborative inquiry: New challenges for school leaders. *International Journal of Leadership in Education. 3*(3), 225–238.

Fichtman Dana, N., Thomas, C., & Boynton, S. (2011). *Inquiry: A districtwide approach to staff and student learning.* Corwin: Thousand Oaks, CA.

Fisher, D., Frey, N., & Pumpian, I. (2012). *How to create a culture of achievement in your school and classroom.* Association for Supervision and Curriculum Development: Alexandria, VA.

Fullan, M. (2008). *The six secrets of change: What the best leaders do to help their organizations survive and thrive.* Jossey-Bass: San Francisco, CA.

Fullan, M. (2011). *Change leader: Learning to Do What Matters Most.* Jossey-Bass: San Francisco, CA.

Galligan, G. (2011). *Collaborative inquiry, teacher efficacy, and writing achievement* (Unpublished dissertation). Arizona State University.

Gallimore, R., Ermeling, B., Saunders, W., & Goldenberg, C. (2009). Moving the learning of teaching closer to practice: Teacher education implications of school-based inquiry teams. *The Elementary School Journal, 109*(5), 537–553.

Garmston, R. (2012). *Unlocking group potential to improve schools.* Corwin: Thousand Oaks, CA.

Gawande, A. (2009). *The checklist manifesto: How to get things right.* Metropolitan Books: New York, NY.

Given, H., Kuh, L., LeeKeenan, D., Mardell, B., Redditt, S., & Twombly, S. (2010). Changing school culture: Using documentation to support collaborative inquiry. *Theory into Practice, 49,* 36–46.

Gladwell, M. (2002). *The tipping point: How little things can make a big difference.* Back Bay Books: New York, NY.

Goddard, R., Hoy, W., & Woolfolk Hoy, A. (2003). Collective efficacy beliefs: Theoretical developments, empirical evidence, and future directions. *Education Researcher, 33*(3), 3–13.

Hargreaves, A., & Fullan, M. (2012). *Professional capital: Transforming teaching in every school.* Teachers' College Press: New York, NY.

Hattie, J. (2009). *Visible learning: A synthesis of over 800 meta-analyses relating to achievement.* Routledge: New York, NY.

Hattie, J. (2012). *Visible learning for teachers: Maximizing impact on learning.* Routledge: New York, NY.

Hattie, J. (2015). *What works best in education: The politics of collaborative expertise.* Pearson: London, England.

Hattie, J., & Yates, G. (2014). *Visible learning and the science of how we learn.* Routledge: New York, NY.

Heifetz, R., Grashow, A., & Linsky, M. (2009). *The practice of adaptive leadership: Tools and tactics for changing your organization and the world.* Harvard Business Press: Boston, MA.

Heifetz, R., & Laurie, D. (1997). The work of leadership. *Harvard Business Review, 75*(1), 124–134.

Heller, R., & Greenleaf, C. (2007). *Literacy instruction in the content areas: Getting to the core of middle and high school improvement.* Alliance for Excellent Education: Washington, DC.

Henson, R. (2001). *The effect of participation in teacher research professional development on teacher efficacy and empowerment.* Paper presented at the Annual Meeting of the Mid-South Educational Research Association.

Hirsh, S., & Killion, J. (2007). *The learning educator: A new era of professional learning.* National Staff Development Council: Oxford, OH.

Horton, J., & Martin, B. (2013). The role of the district administration within Professional Learning Communities. *International Journal of Leadership in Education, 16*(1), 55–70.

Irvin, T. (1999). *Theory as espoused and practiced by a high school English teacher: Staying with the tried and true.* Paper presented at the Annual Meeting of the Mid-South Educational Research Association.

James, M., & Pedder, D. (2006). Beyond method: Assessment and learning practices and values. *The Curriculum Journal, 17*(2), 109–138.

Johnson, S. (2012). *The impact of collaborative structures on perceived collective efficacy* (Unpublished dissertation). Notre Dame of Maryland University.

Katz, S., & Dack, L. A. (2013). *Intentional interruption: Breaking down learning barriers to transform professional practice.* Corwin: Thousand Oaks, CA.

Katz, S., Earl, L., & Ben Jaafar, S. (2009). *Building and connecting learning communities: The power of networks for school improvement.* Corwin: Thousand Oaks, CA.

Kazemi, E., & Franke, M. (2004). Teacher learning in mathematics: Using student work to promote collective inquiry. *Journal of Mathematics Teacher Education, 7*, 203–235.

Knight, J. (n.d.). *Another freakin' thing we've got to do: Teacher perceptions of professional development.* University of Kansas Center for Research on Learning.

Knight, J. (2011). *Unmistakable impact: A partnership approach for dramatically improving instruction.* Corwin: Thousand Oaks, CA.

Langer, G., & Colton, A. (2005). Looking at student work. *Education Leadership, 62*(5), 22–26.

Learning Forward (n.d.). Retrieved from http://www.learningforward.org/standards/index.cfm.

Lee, I. (2009). Ten mismatches between teachers' beliefs and written feedback practice. *ELT Journal, 63*(1).

Lieberman, A., & Miller, A. (2004). *Teacher leadership.* Jossey-Bass: San Francisco, CA.

Lin, X., Schwartz, D., & Hatano, G. (2005). Toward teachers' adaptive metacognition. *Educational Psychologist, 40*(4), 245–255.

Lipton, L., & Wellman, B. (2011). *Leading groups: Effective strategies for building professional community.* Miravia: Sherman, CT.

Little, J. W. (1982). Norms of collegiality and experimentation: Workplace conditions of school success. *American Educational Research Journal, 19*(3), 325–340.

Little, J. W. (1990). The persistence of privacy: Autonomy and initiative in teachers' professional relations. *Teacher College Record, 91*(4), 509–536.

Little, J. W. (2002). Professional community and the problem of high school reform. *International Journal of Education Research, 37*, 693–714.

Marzano, R., Waters, T., & McNulty, B. (2005). *School leadership that works.* Association for Supervision and Curriculum Development: Alexandria, VA.

Moolenaar, A., Sleegers, P., & Daly, A. (2012). Teaming up: Linking collaboration networks, collective efficacy, and student achievement. *Teaching and Teacher Education, 28*, 251–262.

Nelson, T. (2008). Teachers' collaborative inquiry and professional growth: Should we be optimistic? *Science Teacher Education,* Retrieved from Wiley Periodicals, http://onlinelibrary.wiley.com/doi/10.1002/sce.20302/abstract

Nelson, T., Perkins, M., & Hathorn, T. (2008). A culture of collaborative inquiry: Learning to develop and support professional learning communities. *Teachers College Record, 110*(6), 1269–1303.

Nelson, T., Deuel, A., Slavit, D., & Kennedy, A. (2010). Leading deep conversations in collaborative inquiry groups. *The Clearing House, 83*, 175–179.

Pink. D. (2009). *Drive: The surprising truth about what motivates us.* Penguin Books: New York, NY.

Quinn, J. (2015). Engaging thought leaders: An interview with Joanne Quinn—New pedagogies for deep learning. *Learning Forward Ontario Newsletter, 7*(1), 6–7.

Reeves, D. (2008). *Reframing teacher leadership to improve your school.* Association for Supervision and Curriculum Development: Alexandria, VA.

Reeves, D. (2010). *Transforming professional development into student results.* Association for Supervision and Curriculum Development: Alexandria, VA.

Reeves, D. (2011). *Finding your leadership focus: What matters most for student results.* Teachers College Press: New York, NY.

Rincon-Gallardo, S., & Fullan, M. (2016). Essential features of effective networks in education, *Journal of Professional Capital and Community, 1*(1).

Roblin, N., & Margalef, L. (2013). Learning from dilemmas: Teacher professional development through collaborative action and reflection. *Teachers and Teaching: Theory and Practice, 19*(1), 18–32.

Schön, D. (1983). *The reflective practitioner: How professionals think in action.* Basic Books: New York, NY.

Schoorman, F., Mayer, R., & Davis, J. (2007). An integrative model of organizational trust: Past, present, and future. *Academy of Management Review, 32*(2), 344–354.

Schraw, G., & Moshman, D. (1995). Metacognitive theories. *Educational Psychology Review, 7*(4), 351–371.

Scott, S. (2004). *Fierce conversations: Achieving success at work & in life, one conversation at a time.* Berkley Publishing Group: New York, NY.

Senge, P. (1990). *The fifth discipline. The art and practice of the learning organization.* Random House: London, England.

Senge, P., Scharmer, C., Jaworski, J., & Flowers, B. (2004). *Presence: An exploration of profound change in people, organizations, and society.* Double Day: New York, NY.

Shanahan, T., & Shanahan, C. (2008). Teaching disciplinary literacy to adolescents: Rethinking content-area literacy. *Harvard Educational Review, 78*(1), 40–59.

Sparks, D. (2007). *Leading for results: Transforming teaching, learning, and relationships in schools.* Corwin: Thousand Oaks, CA.

Spillane, J. (2006). *Distributed leadership.* Jossey-Bass: San Francisco, CA.

Stanley, A. (2011). Professional development within collaborative teacher study groups: Pitfalls and promises. *Arts Education Review, 112,* 71–78.

Stein, S., & Book, H. (2006). *The EQ edge: Emotional intelligence and your success.* Jossey-Bass: San Francisco, CA.

Stewart, W. (2015). *Leave research to the academics.* Downloaded from https://www.tes.com/news/school-news/breaking-news/leave-research-academics-john-hattie-tells-teachers

Sylwester, R. (1994). How emotions affect learning. *Educational Leadership, 52*(2), 14–19.

Timperley, H., Kaser, L., & Halbert, J. (2014). *A framework for transforming learning in schools: Innovation and the spiral of inquiry.* Seminar Series 234. Centre for Strategic Education. Melbourne.

Timperley, H., Wilson, A., Barrar, H., & Fung, I. (2007). *Teacher Professional Learning and Development: Best evidence synthesis iteration (BES).* Educational Practice Series, 18. University of Auckland, New Zealand.

Tough, P. (2012). *How children succeed: Grit, curiosity, and the hidden power of character.* Houghton Mifflin Harcourt: New York, NY.

Tschannen-Moran, M. (2013). Healthy relationships: The foundation of a positive school climate. *In Conversation, 4*(3), 1–14.

Voelkel Jr., R. (2011). *A case study of the relationship between collective efficacy and professional learning communities.* (Unpublished dissertation). University of California, San Diego, California State University, San Marcos.

Walsh, J., & Sattes, B. (2010). *Leading through quality questioning: Creating capacity, commitment, and community.* Corwin: Thousand Oaks, CA.

Watkins, C. (n.d.). Learners in the driving seat. Leading learning pedagogy. *School Leadership Today*, 1.2, 28–31.

Wheatley, M. (2002). *Turning to one another: Simple conversations to restore hope to the future*. Berrett-Koehler: San Francisco, CA.

Wood, E., Woloshyn, V., & Willoughby, T. (Eds.). (1995). *Cognitive strategy instruction for middle and high schools*. Brookline Books: Cambridge, MA.

Zumbrunn, S., Tadlock, J., & Roberts, E. (2011). *Encouraging self-regulated learning in the classroom: A review of the literature*. Metropolitan Educational Research Consortium: Virginia Commonwealth University. Retrieved from http://www.academia.edu/2527080/Encouraging_Self-Regulated_Learning_in_the_Classroom_A_Review_of_the_Literature.

Index

Achievement. *See* Student learning and achievement
Achinstein, B., 91
Affective student-learning needs, 35–38, 36 (box), 38 (box)
See also Student learning and achievement
Allen, Becky, 8 (box)
Angelle, P., 22
Argyris, C., 10, 50, 65

Bader Primary School, 59 (box)
Balen, Julie, 12–13 (box)
Ball, D., 13, 14
Barrar, H., 6, 14
Battaglia, C., 18, 22, 24
Belief systems, 58
Ben Jaafar, S., 10, 11, 14, 23, 33
Bernhardt, V., 54, 56
Book, H., 36
Bushe, G., 25, 45, 92, 99, xi

Cardwork map
    of adoption of collaborative inquiry, 17 (figure)
    elements in, xi
    of establishing focus, 32 (figure)
    of impact assessment, 52 (figure)
    of professional learning culture, 73 (figure)
    of transformative professional learning, 2 (figure)
"Cardwork Strategy" (Bushe), xi
Causal-Loop Diagram, 68–69
Chaffee, Marty, 23–24 (box)
Chinn, Patricia, 24 (box)
City, E., 45, 92
Classroom environment, 19
    See also School culture
Coburn, C., 18–19, 24, 98

Cognitive student-learning needs, 39–40, 40 (box)
    See also Student learning and achievement
Cohen, D., 13, 14
Collaboration, online spaces for, 94–95, 95–96 (box)
Collaborative Inquiry for Educators, 6
Collaborative inquiry framework overview, 6–8, 7 (figure)
Collaborative inquiry process
    adaptive challenges and, 5, 5 (table)
    administrative leadership, 22–24
    benefits of, 16
    characteristics of, 11–12 (table)
    conflict, role of, 91–92
    dissemination strategies, 26–27, 93–98
    effectiveness and impact of, 4, 63–65, 64 (figure), 71–72
    focus determination, 32–34
    framework of, 6–8, 7 (figure)
    goal cohesiveness, 25–26, 45
    group-generated questions, 62–63
    inquiry question, formulation of, 44, 57–58
    Partnership Principles, 81–83
    redefintion of scale, 18–19
    reflection, 67–69, 68 (figure), 69 (figure), 70 (figure)
    skilled facilitation, 27–29, 45 (box), 60–61, 67, 85–86, 86 (table)
    teacher leadership, 10, 14, 20–22
    teaching efficacy and, 4
    theory of action development, 44–51
    trust development, 83–85
    voluntary participation, 20
    See also Facilitator skills; Team development; Theory of action
Collective efficacy. *See* Efficacy, teacher
Colton, A., 61

Conflict, 91–92
Copland, M., 21
Csikszentmihalyi, M., 11

Dack, L. A., 2, 11, 15, 45, 50, 75
Darling-Hammond, L., 13, 36
Data. *See* Student assessment
Davis, J., 84
Derrington, M., 22
Deuel, A., 62
Dissemination of knowledge, 26–27
    documentation, 93
    facilitator summit, 97
    learning fairs, 96–97
    network establishment, 93–95
    publications and presentations, 97–98
Double-loop learning, 50–51
Dweck, C., 10

Earl, L., 10, 11, 14, 23, 91
Eells, R., 3
Efficacy, teacher
    collective, 3–4, 10, 18, 22, 26, 93
    student achievement and, 14, 18, 53
Elmore, R., 45, 68, 92
Emihovich, C., 18, 22, 24
Emotions, 35–38, 36 (box)
English language learners (ELLs), 87 (box)
Ermeling, B., 4, 43
Experimental research, 9
Extrinsic rewards, 37–38

Facilitator skills
    capacity building, 85–86
    guidance on protocols, 60–61
    importance of, 28–29
    inquiry question development, 45 (box)
    primary roles, 27–28, 97–98
    reflection of experiences, 67–68
    trust development, 61
    See also Team development
Feasey, Simon, 59 (box)
Fiarman, S., 45, 92
Fisher, D., 97
Flowers, B., 68
Franke, M., 59
Frey, N., 97
Fullan, M., 4, 14, 45, 46, 47, 50, 94
Fung, I., 6, 14

Gallimore, R., 4, 43
Garmston, R., 68, 69, 71
Given, H., 59, 87
Gladwell, M., 26

Goldenberg, C., 4, 43
Google Docs, 95
Grashow, A., 5
Greenleaf, C., 43
Group development. *See* Team
    development

Halbert, J., 6, 14, 42
Hall, Gillian, 87 (box)
Hargreaves, A., 4, 14, 94
Hatano, G., 41
Hathorn, T., 89
Hattie, J., 3, 9, 10, 14, 38, 39, 40, 66
Heifetz, R., 5
Heller, R., 43
Homb, Sandy, 8 (box)
Hopkins Public Schools, 8–9 (box)

Impact assessment. *See* Student assessment
Imposter syndrome, 11
Intrinsic rewards, 38
Irvin, T., 66

James, M., 69
Jaworski, J., 68
Johnson, S., 26

Kaser, L., 6, 14, 42
Katz, S., 2, 10, 11, 14, 23, 33, 45, 50, 75, 91
Kazemi, E., 59
Kennedy, A., 62
Kirsch, E., 36
Knight, J., 74, 80, 81–83, 92
Kuh, L., 59, 87

Langer, G., 61
Leadership
    administrative, 22–24
    facilitator, 27–29, 60–61, 67, 85–86, 97
    shared, 20–22
    teacher, 10, 14
Learning fairs, 96–97
Learning Forward, 75
Lee, I., 66
LeeKeenan, D., 59, 87
Lieberman, A., 14
Lin, X., 41
Linsky, M., 5
Lipton, L., 89, 90
Lit, I., 36
Little, J. W., 13, 43

Maltby, Dean, 95 (box)
Mardell, B., 59, 87

Margalef, L., 60
Marshak, R., 25
Martin, D., 36
Mayer, R., 84
Metacognitive student-learning needs,
    40–42, 42 (box)
    See also Student learning and
        achievement
Miller, A., 14
Mindframes, 10
Motivation, 37–38

Needs-based focus
    cardwork map of, 32 (figure)
    identifying student learning needs,
        33–42
    multidisciplinary teams and, 42–43
    teaching-focus *vs.* learning focus, 34
Nelson, T., 28, 29, 60, 61, 62, 89
Network establishment, 93–95

Oakland Schools, 23–24 (box)
Online communications, 94–95,
    95–96 (box)
Ontario Secondary School Literacy Test
    (OSSLT), 21
Orcutt, S., 36

Partnership Principles
    choice, 81–82
    conflict and, 92
    dialogue, 82–83
    equality, 81
    praxis, 83
    reciprocity, 83
    reflections, 82
    voice, 82
Pedder, D., 69
Perkins, M., 89
Pink, D., 38
Process of reconciliation, 46, 65–67
Professional development *vs.* professional
    learning, 74–77, 76 (table)
Professional learning
    benefits of, 13–15
    challenges in, 11
    and change, 77–78, 78 (table)
    collaborative inquiry framework, 6–8,
        7 (figure)
    collaborative inquiry process overview,
        10–11, 12–13 (table)
    collective efficacy and, 3–4, 14, 18
    commitment to, 78–79
    impacts on student learning, 8–9 (box)

professional capital development, 4
    reflection process, 67–69, 68 (figure),
        69 (figure), 70 (figure)
    schedules and, 26–27
    vs. professional development, 74–77,
        76 (table)
    See also Collaborative inquiry process
Professional relationship development.
    See Partnership Principles
Pumpian, I., 97

Quinn, J., 25

Redditt, S., 59, 87
Reeves, D., 14, 51, 98
Reflection process, 67–69, 68 (figure),
    69 (figure), 70 (figure)
Results Path tool, 63–65, 64 (figure)
Roberts, E., 37
Roblin, N., 60

Saunders, W., 4, 43
Scale, redefinition of, 18–19
Scharmer, C., 68
Schön, D., 10, 50, 65, 67
School culture
    classroom environment, 19
    district cohesiveness and, 25–26
    sustainable improvement of, 59 (box)
    teacher efficacy and, 4, 14, 77
School Effectiveness Framework (SEF), 21
Schoorman, F., 84
Schwartz, D., 41
Scott, S., 71
Senge, P., 68
Shared leadership, 20–22
Simcoe County District School Board,
    95–96 (box)
Simpson, Anita, 95 (box)
The Six Secrets of Change (Fullan), 46
Slavit, D., 62
Sparks, D., 45, 49
Standards for Professional Learning
    (Learning Forward), 75
Stein, S., 36
Strobel, K., 36
Student assessment
    analysis of student work, 59–62
    data collection considerations, 57–61
    demographic data, 55, 55 (box)
    perceptual data, 56, 57 (box)
    Results Path tool and, 63–65, 64 (figure)
    school process data, 56, 56 (box)
    student-learning data, 54, 55 (box)

Student learning and achievement
    affective student-learning needs, 35–38,
        36 (box), 38 (box)
    cognitive student-learning needs, 39–40,
        40 (box)
    competency beliefs, 36 (box)
    metacognitive student-learning needs,
        40–42, 42 (box)
    motivation, 37–38
    teacher efficacy and, 3, 14, 18, 53
    See also Student assessment
Success attributions, 37 (box)
Sylwester, R., 36, 37

Tadlock, J., 37
Teacher effectiveness. *See* Efficacy, teacher
Teacher Professional Learning and
        Development (Timperley, et al.), 14
Team development
    conflict, role of, 91–92
    facilitator knowledge and skills, 86 (figure)
    group norms, 89–91, 90 (table)
    individual stances and, 87, 88 (table)
    rewards and celebrations, 93
    trust development, 60–61, 83–85
    See also Facilitator skills
Teitel, L., 45, 92

Theory of action
    double-loop learning and, 50–51
    effectiveness of, 47–50
    embedded assumptions, 49–50
    if/then statements, 45, 47, 48 (box)
    process of reconciliation and, 46, 65–67
    purpose of, 44–46
Timperley, H., 6, 14, 33, 42
Tough, P., 36
Trust development, 60–61, 83–85
Tschannen-Moran, M., 84
Twombly, S., 59, 87

Value systems, 58
Voelkel, R., Jr., 4

Watkins, C., 66
Wellman, B., 89, 90
Wikwemikong High School, 12–13 (box)
Willoughby, T, 39
Wilson, A., 6, 14
Woloshyn, V., 39
Wood, E., 39

Yates, G., 39

Zumbrunn, S., 37

CORWIN

A SAGE Publishing Company

CORWIN HAS ONE MISSION: to enhance education through intentional professional learning.

We build long-term relationships with our authors, educators, clients, and associations who partner with us to develop and continuously improve the best evidence-based practices that establish and support lifelong learning.

THE PROFESSIONAL LEARNING ASSOCIATION

Learning Forward is a nonprofit, international membership association of learning educators committed to one vision in K–12 education: Excellent teaching and learning every day. To realize that vision, Learning Forward pursues its mission to build the capacity of leaders to establish and sustain highly effective professional learning. Information about membership, services, and products is available from www.learningforward.org.

Solutions you want. Experts you trust. Results you need.

Author Consulting

On-site professional learning with sustainable results! Let us help you design a professional learning plan to meet the unique needs of your school or district. www.corwin.com/pd

Institutes

Corwin Institutes provide collaborative learning experiences that equip your team with tools and action plans ready for immediate implementation. www.corwin.com/institutes

eCourses

Practical, flexible online professional learning designed to let you go at your own pace. www.corwin.com/ecourses

Read2Earn

Did you know you can earn graduate credit for reading this book? Find out how: www.corwin.com/read2earn